Y0-CAG-032

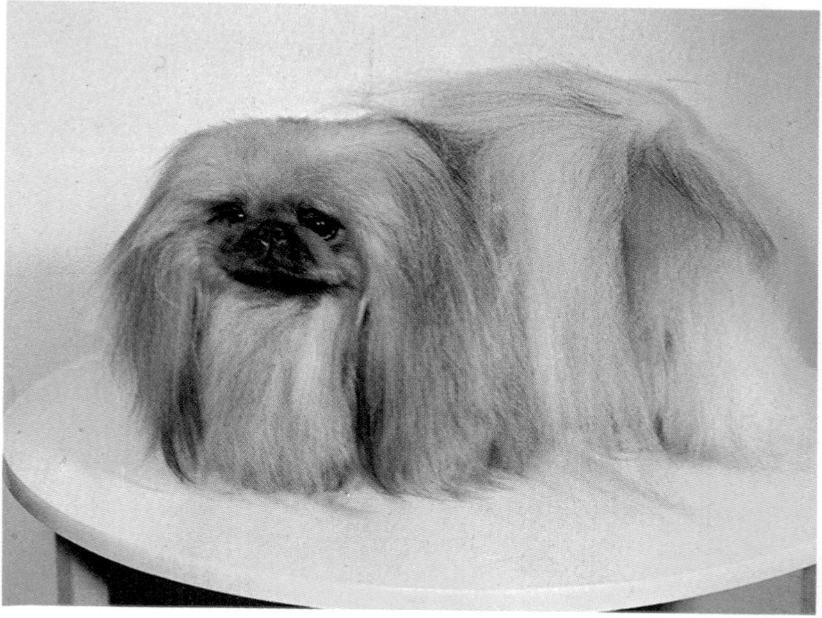

DANVILLE PUBLIC LIBRARY
DANVILLE, INDIANA

PEKINGESE
KW-095

# PEKINGESE

BEVERLY PISANO

*Their petite size and noble dispositions made the Pekingese especially popular with the emperor, who often would carry his favorite Peke in his sleeve while he went about his daily business. Owner, Shirley Schwartz.*

068883

# Contents



8.00

**Title page:** *The unique personality of the Pekingese—confident and somewhat haughty—has remained a point of intrigue and delight for dog fanciers everywhere. Owner, Jeanine Joyal.*

**Photography:** *Isabelle Francais, Herrlick Hamburg, Ron Moat, Vince Serbin, Sally Anne Thompson, Louise Van der Meid, and Ake Wintzell.*

**Drawings:** *Scott Boldt, Richard Davis, AnnMarie Freda, Scott Holwick, E. Michael Horn, Andrew Prendimano, John Quinn, and Alexandra Suchenka.*

The text of this book is the result of the joint effort of the author and the editorial staff of T.F.H. Publications, Inc., which is the originator of all sections of the book except the chapters dealing with the history, character, breed standard, and grooming. Additionally, the portrayal of canine pet products in this book is for general instructive value only; the appearance of such products does not necessarily constitute an endorsement by the author, the publisher, or the owners of the dogs portrayed in this book.

t.f.h.

**1995 Edition**

Distributed in the UNITED STATES to the Pet Trade by T.F.H. Publications, Inc., One T.F.H. Plaza, Neptune City, NJ 07753; distributed in the UNITED STATES to the Bookstore and Library Trade by National Book Network, Inc. 4720 Boston Way, Lanham MD 20706; in CANADA to the Pet Trade by H & L Pet Supplies Inc., 27 Kingston Crescent, Kitchener, Ontario N2B 2T6; Rolf C. Hagen Ltd., 3225 Sartelon Street, Montreal 382 Quebec; in CANADA to the Book Trade by Vanwell Publishing Ltd., 1 Northrup Crescent, St. Catharines, Ontario L2M 6P5 ; in ENGLAND by T.F.H. Publications, PO Box 15, Waterlooville PO7 6BQ; in AUSTRALIA AND THE SOUTH PACIFIC by T.F.H. (Australia), Pty. Ltd., Box 149, Brookvale 2100 N.S.W., Australia; in NEW ZEALAND by Brooklands Aquarium Ltd. 5 McGiven Drive, New Plymouth, RD1 New Zealand; in Japan by T.F.H. Publications, Japan—Jiro Tsuda, 10-12-3 Ohjidai, Sakura, Chiba 285, Japan; in SOUTH AFRICA by Lopis (Pty) Ltd., P.O. Box 39127, Booysens, 2016, Johannesburg, South Africa. Published by T.F.H. Publications, Inc.

MANUFACTURED IN THE UNITED STATES OF AMERICA
BY T.F.H. PUBLICATIONS, INC.

# Introducing the Pekingese

## HISTORY

This intriguing little breed from the Orient, long a favorite with royalty, has become just as popular in our society today as it was in the imperial courts of the ancients. It is a charming canine companion who offers its master an abundance of loving affection and amusing antics.

The Pekingese, truly an "imperial" dog, has a history that takes it back to ancient times, as far back, some say, as 2000 B.C. For centuries, the Pekingese, or "Peke," was worshipped in the temples of China, and it was a custom of the emperor to select four Pekes who were to become his "bodyguards." These four Pekes would precede the emperor to the Chamber of Ceremonials on occasions of state; two of them announcing his approach at correct intervals with sharp, piercing barks, the other two daintily holding the hem of his royal robe in their mouths. Theft of or damage to one of the royal dogs was considered to be a crime punishable by death.

There are myriad legends concerning the origin of the Pekingese. Among the most colorful ones is that of the romance of "the Lion and the Marmoset."

One day while the mighty king of all beasts, the Lion, was walking through the Magic Forest, he stopped by a pool to rest and have a cool drink from the pool. As he stepped to the edge of the pool, he saw the reflection of a beautiful little Marmoset monkey perched in the tree nearby. Immediately he found himself madly in love with the exquisite creature, but after some meditation, he became very sad. He realized how large and mighty he was and how tiny and delicate the little Marmoset looked. But as the days passed, he still could think only of his love for the Marmoset. The Fairy Godmother came upon the Lion, and seeing him so downcast, asked if she could help him. After listening to his story, the Fairy Godmother said, "Oh King of All Beasts, I will grant your wish." The Fairy Godmother waved her magic wand and the Lion was made as small as the little Marmoset. To this day, the little monkey-faced Pekingese has some of the characteristics of the lion about him—the regal bearing and profuse mane.

As to the *true* origin of the Pekingese, we find that the name of "Pekingese" has been given to the rough-coated dog whose smooth-coated relative has been known as the Chinese pug dog. Opportunities for research in

**Facing page:** *Legend and myth trace the Pekingese's origins to a magical cross between the Lion and the Marmoset monkey. Whatever the origin, the Peke is a fascinating and wonderful creature!*

*High Foo Yung Ku Zette perhaps bears a resemblance to the dark sable, black-masked dog that Admiral Lord John Jay brought to England in the early 1860s.*

bygone Chinese lore have been very limited, but there is sufficient evidence to establish what we have stated as authentic.

In the Metropolitan Museum of Art in New York, there are many Chinese porcelains, the Bishop collections of jade, and the Pierpont Morgan collections, all of which contain data regarding these dogs. The oldest of these is the carved crystal in the Bishop collection entitled "Lions," a Pekingese bitch with two puppies. Each has a pendant or drop ear and a tail plumed over the back. The heads are massive and flat across the top of the skull; the muzzle is short but very full. The mane is indicated as profuse. The date on this piece is given as the Ming Dynasty, 1368-1644. In the same Bishop collection, there can be found a dog and puppy, also called "Lions"; the date for this is 1736-1795.

The Morgan collection is all porcelain or earthenware. The porcelain pieces show the best illustrations of Pekingese dogs to be found, with beautiful plates having a pattern of the Pekingese in "biscuit color." On other porcelain plates are two Pekingese dogs with black and white coloring; on another the coloring is principally white. These plates are also placed in the 1736-1795 collection.

Although the circle of

information is very limited, the Pekingese, both rough and smooth, were known to England a century ago, specimens having been brought to that country as loot from the imperial palaces.

In October, 1860, four small Pekingese were presented to Queen Victoria by Lieutenant Dunne. However, three of these dogs found their way to the "Goodwood" Castle, property of the Duke of Gordon and Lord John Hay. It was from these dogs that the English get their "Goodwood" line of Pekingese.

## THE PEKE COMES TO AMERICA

In 1898 the first Pekingese came to America. They were admitted to A.K.C. registry in 1906, and to show classification in 1907. The Pekingese Club of America was formed in 1909 and gave its first Specialty Show in January, 1911.

Pekes have continued to capture the fancy of American dog lovers, and as testimony to their popularity, they now occupy a high ranking on the AKC's registrations listing—being in the top 25.

*In any breed, uniformity and consistency are of utmost importance. The Pekingese has remained considerably uniform for generations.*

**CHARACTER**

Pekingese are the aristocrats of dogdom, with many different characteristics in one little parcel. A fascinating breed, they are lovable, haughty, and bold, with a quaintness that is irresistible. These small companions are suited to most environments, and are loyal to child and adult alike.

Having lovable dispositions, Pekes are not bad tempered, as some people have been led to believe. In fact, they are quite anxious to please. However, many are quite haughty with strangers, for they seem to know they are of royal ancestry and merit due respect from everyone! While they may be resentful if strangers make advances first, if you give them time they will make friends. They will come to you freely when they are convinced of your good intentions. Then, when you make a return visit, they will greet you as if they had always known you.

Pekingese are obedient little dogs, and are easy to train. Speak to them in a gentle but firm tone and they are willing to do anything for you. Kindness goes a long way with these royal little dogs.

The Pekingese is often called the Lion Dog, and with his flowing mane and pear-shaped body he does resemble the king of the forest. If he should come face to face with his namesake, he may well be undaunted, for he has no

*Pekingese are obedient, gentle and lovable. They can also be very children-oriented dogs, for frolicking and playing in the backyard are among the Peke's favorite pastimes.*

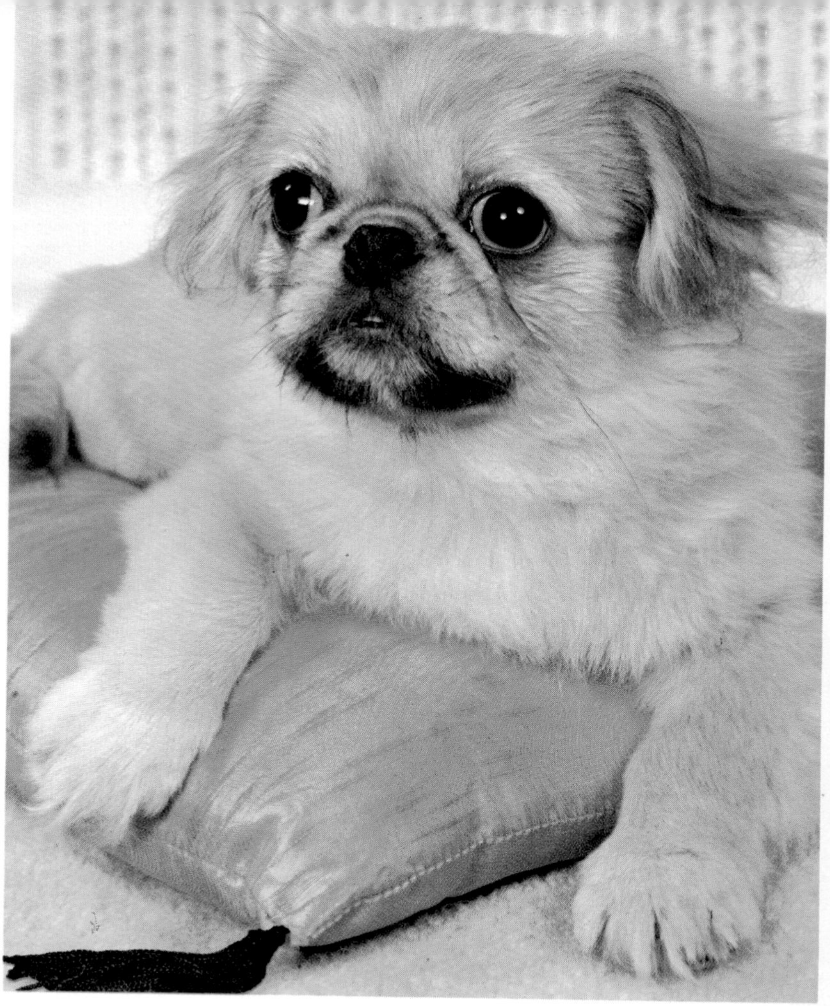

*Although hailed by dogdom as an "imperial" dog, the Pekingese is hardly the lazy, pillow-sitting dog. This Peke, however, does not seem too concerned with breaking the stereotype.*

fear of animals many times his size. Pekingese make wonderful watchdogs who bark at any strange noises, but never bark just to be barking.

They love to romp and play; they can take long walks or sit quietly by your side for many hours, happy just to be near you. They love to go places and are a source of great fun. Alert, seeing everything that is going on around them, many delight in watching television!

Pekingese are rather jealous by nature and like all the attention they can have. Yet, they can easily be trained to share this affection with a cat or another dog. Once they become friends, they will sleep and eat together, sharing the affection of their master and mistress.

Pekes are hardy little dogs with a stamina much greater than their size. The Pekingese is anything but a silk pillow dog, as he is so often pictured. He can romp and play for a long while without tiring easily.

These tiny dogs have clean habits, which means that they are easily housebroken. Most Pekingese are very fastidious, unhappy if their lovely coats become soiled, delighted after they are washed or groomed. Some show their pleasure at being groomed by rolling over on their backs so their stomach coat can be gently brushed.

Quite the show-offs when they want to attract your attention, Pekes will sit up, wave their paws and "speak." They use their paws in play a great deal like a kitten; in fact, tricks seem to be second nature to them, and puppies barely past weaning age will sit up to attract attention.

Their characters are to a great extent formed by their owners, for they seem to sense your every mood. Many times a little Pekingese with his great devotion has eased the pain of illness or another's grief. And many Peke owners have said that their loyal companion carried them through an almost unbearable time.

Usually there is one member of the family that the pet is more fond of and will obey more readily. Occasionally you will find a Pekingese that gives all of his affection to one member of the family, simply ignoring everyone else when this person is present. But when this favorite is absent, he will be very friendly with the rest of the family. Then again there will be one who is very loving and friendly with all members of the household, but when company arrives, he will completely ignore the family and give all his attention to the guests. Maybe he is trying to be a good host. One fascination of the Pekingese character is that you never quite know exactly what they are thinking.

Pekingese come in many colors, ranging from whites, creams, many shades of fawn, reds, sables, and brindles to blacks and blacks with tan, gray, fawn or red markings.

**Facing page:** *Given the opportunity to run about the backyard, your Pekingese will show you how much he enjoys exercise and play.*

### THE IMPORTANCE OF BREED STANDARDS

If you plan to enter your Pekingese into show competition, you should become thoroughly familiar with the official standard of the national club under which your dog is registered, and also with those standards of other jurisdictions if you are considering international exposure for your Pekingese.

Even if you do not desire to show or breed your Pekingese (and instead want simply a beloved household pet), you may indeed be interested in knowing about those attributes that exemplify the perfect Pekingese.

### AMERICAN AND BRITISH STANDARDS

The official standards as approved by the American Kennel Club and the Kennel Club (Great Britain) have very much in common. Despite differences in wording, both call for essentially the same requirements. It must be noted, however, that the British standard calls for maximum weights to be only 11 pounds for dogs and 12 pounds for bitches.

For the sake of brevity, we are including only the American Kennel Club standard in this book. If your Pekingese is registered with a different national club, write to that club and request a copy of the official standard. Considering that these standards have a tendency to change in the way they are worded from time to time, serious show persons are advised to contact their local club for the most up-to-date standard available.

### THE PEKINGESE STANDARD (AKC)

***Expression:*** Must suggest the Chinese origin of the Pekingese in its quaintness and individuality, resemblance to the lion in directions and independence and should imply courage, boldness, self-esteem and combativeness rather than prettiness, daintiness or delicacy.

***Skull:*** Massive, broad, wide and flat between the ears (not dome-shaped), wide between the eyes. ***Nose:*** Black, broad, very short and flat. ***Eyes:*** Large, dark, prominent, round, lustrous. ***Stop:*** Deep. ***Ears:*** Heart-shaped, not set too high, leather never long enough to come below the muzzle, nor carried erect, but rather drooping, long feather. ***Muzzle:*** Wrinkled, very short and broad, not overshot nor pointed. Strong, broad underjaw, teeth not to show.

***Shape of Body:*** Heavy in front, well-sprung ribs, broad chest, falling away lighter behind, lion-like. Back, level. Not too long in body; allowance made for longer body in bitch. ***Legs:*** Short forelegs, bones of forearm, bowed, firm at shoulder; hind legs, lighter but firm and well shaped. ***Feet:*** Flat, toes, turned out, not

*This beautiful chun red bitch is High Foo Zinnia of Hedingham. Her consistent impeccable type and undeniable beauty have made her a champion of champions; she has more than 200 awards to her credit. Owner, Peggy Winston.*

round, should stand well up on feet, not on ankles.

***Action:*** Fearless, free and strong, with slight roll.

***Coat, Feather, and Condition:*** Long with thick undercoat, straight and flat, not curly nor wavy, rather coarse, but soft; feather on thighs, legs, tail and toes long and profuse. ***Mane:*** Profuse, extending beyond the shoulder blades, forming ruff or frill round the neck.

***Color:*** All colors are allowable. Red, fawn, black, black and tan, sable, brindle, white and parti-color well defined; black masks and spectacles around the eyes, with lines to ears are desirable. ***Definition of a Parti-Color Pekingese:*** The coloring of a parti-colored dog must be broken on the body. No large portion of any one color should exist. White should be shown on the saddle. A dog of any solid color with white feet and chest is not a parti-color.

***Tail:*** Set high; lying well over back to either side; long, profuse, straight feather.

***Size:*** Being a toy dog, medium size preferred, providing type and points are not sacrificed; extreme limit, 14 pounds.

FAULTS

*Protruding tongue, badly blemished eye, overshot, wry mouth.*

DISQUALIFICATIONS

*Weight: over 14 pounds.*
*Dudley nose.*

*As its name suggests, the Pekingese is a breed which finds its origin in the Orient, where it was much revered and loved by the royal family. A Plutuo dog.*

# Grooming the Peke

A well-groomed Pekingese is a beautiful sight to behold, with his glossy coat, long plume tail and fringes. Pekingese stay as nature intended them to, with no cropping of ears or docking of tails. The only trimming done is to whiskers on the muzzle, and then only if the dog is to be entered at a show. The whiskers are clipped close the day of the show, with blunt-end scissors, to protect the eyes from injury should the dog move suddenly or give a struggle. Clipping the whiskers gives a neater, smoother finish to the muzzle.

Grooming should start as soon as the new pet is settled in his home. The most important part of the grooming equipment is the brush, and it should be used every day if possible. Genuine bristle brushes are preferred, especially those that are not too stiff. A coarse-toothed steel comb should be used just to work any tangles out, not for rough combing that might pull out the coat.

Place a blanket or rug on the table on which you'll groom your pet. Start with your pet on his back, so the "underneath" coat can be groomed first. If the coat is soiled, wring a cloth out in warm water and rub the soiled places, sprinkle with talcum powder and rub it well into the coat. Now rub dry with a towel and then brush briskly until each hair seems to stand alone. If the coat is not soiled, just brush well.

Turn your pet over and stand him firmly on his feet. This will accustom your dog to posing on a table as would be required at a dog show. If in the future you decide to show your Peke, this will be an important part of his training. Brush briskly, using light strokes against the lay of the coat. Start at the back of the neck and brush forward from the skin to the end of the hair and always toward the head. By the time you have covered the whole body, each hair will be glossy and clean.

Lift the ear and gently brush the hair underneath and in back of it. Now take your steel comb and gently work out any tangles. Don't ever cut out the tangles that form behind the ears or on any part of the coat, as this will leave an ugly, ragged place that is not at all becoming to a lovely little Pekingese.

Clean the ears gently inside (not probing too far into the ear) with a damp cloth and carefully remove any wax accumulation with a cotton swab, then dust a pinch of medicated powder into each ear. While you have the ear pulled up, place it flat against the head and brush the fringe on the edge of it,

**Facing page:** *In order to keep your Pekingese's coat in top condition, regular brushing and grooming are essential.*

let the ear drop in place and brush the fringe down and a little forward to make a lovely frame for the face.

The fringes on the legs are to be brushed as well, and if necessary they can be combed. This can be done easily while the dog is lying on his back for grooming underneath.

Hold the tail out in back and comb any tangles; then place the plume over the back and brush gently toward the head until it resembles a silken fan. Brush the hair flat on the top of the skull to give the proper flatness between the ears. The skirts (bitches-females) or pants (dogs-males) can be lifted and held with one hand while a little at a time is brushed down from underneath until they are all brushed.

Dampen a cloth with warm water and wash the face, being careful to wash under the wrinkle and drying it well, as a damp wrinkle can become very sore. Dust a little medicated powder under the wrinkle to keep it dry.

Drop any good eye wash, preferably one that your veterinarian recommends, into each eye to wash away any dust or hair that may have accumulated during the grooming of your pet.

Keep the toenails trimmed or they will grow long, sometimes curving right back into the pad of the foot, causing extreme pain and great difficulty in walking. An eye can be badly damaged by an uncut toenail. For this purpose, a special clipper for dogs can be obtained from your retail pet supplier.

*Bathe your Peke only when absolutely necessary. Bathing him too often is a sure way to dry out his coat and cause his skin to become scaly.*

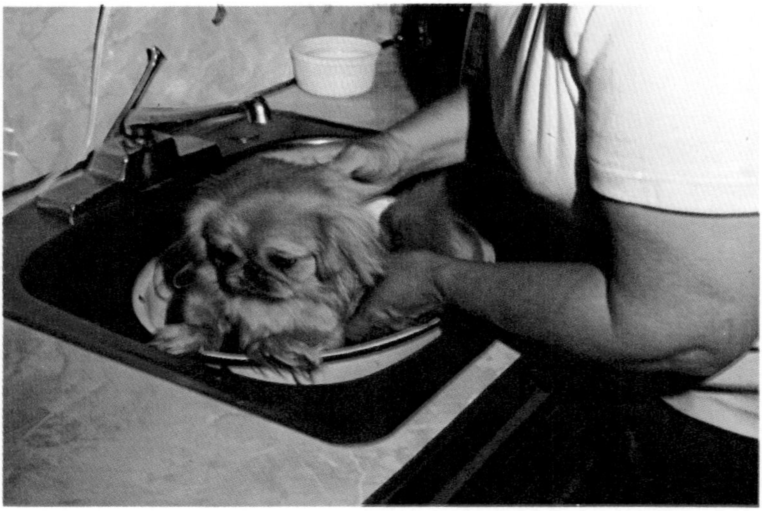

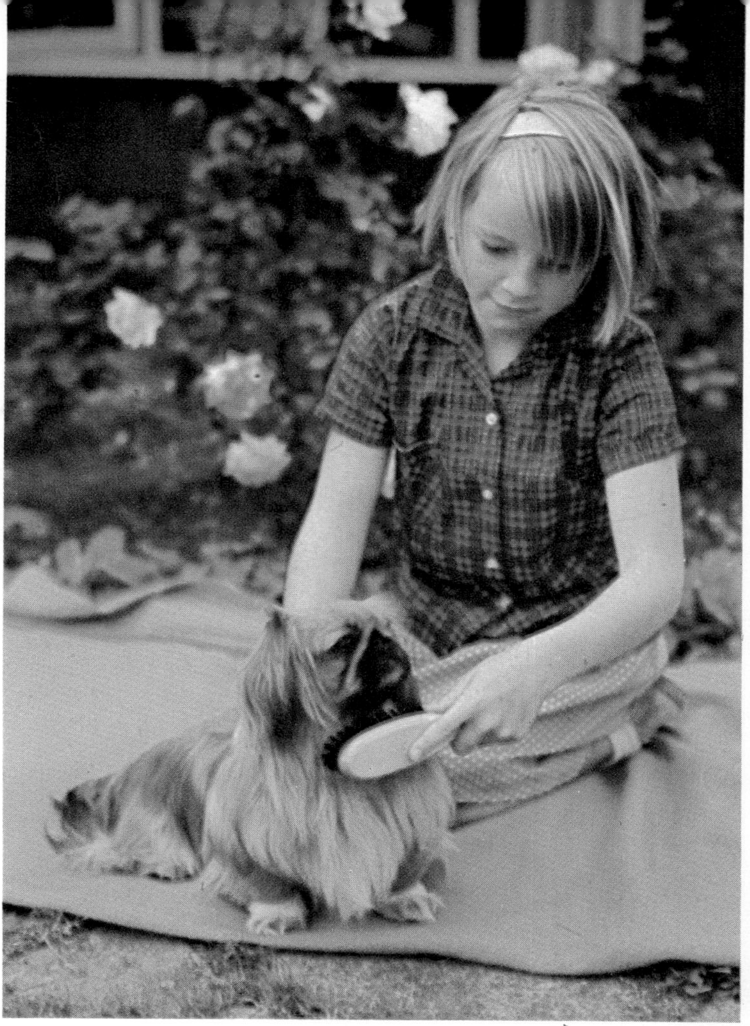

*Brushing your dog is of utmost importance, for it helps reduce shedding and keeps the coat looking its best. Do not hesitate to brush your dog when he is shedding—your efforts can only help his new coat to grow in faster and fuller.*

See to it that you don't cut too far down and injure the "quick," which will cause pain and bleeding. Have your vet show you the proper way to clip the nails. Trim the hair between the pads of the feet, for accumulated dirt there will often cause soreness. Dust a little powder between the pads after cleaning and drying them.

Examine your pet's mouth at least once a week, and clean out anything that might have lodged between the teeth. Take a soft damp cloth and wipe the teeth clean. Some Pekes do not object to a small tooth brush. If tartar forms, have it removed by your veterinarian.

To keep your pet free from fleas and other such parasites, a liquid solution rubbed into the coat is better than powder. Because of the Pekes' flat noses and large eyes, a powder can be harmful unless used very carefully. Flea powder also tends to dry the skin.

Don't bathe your Pekingese unless absolutely necessary, as soap and water baths take the oil out of the coat and cause it to be flat and lifeless. It also can cause the skin to become dry and scaly. A towel dampened in lukewarm water and rubbed briskly all over your pet and right down to the skin will clean the coat and skin and keep it in much better condition. A brisk rub with a dry towel, a good brushing and your pet is as clean as he would have been with a soap and water bath and much more beautiful, with a sparkle and gloss to the coat!

The only time a good bath is recommended is before a show appearance, or after your pet has completed a shedding of his coat. As soon as you notice your Peke starting to shed, brush and comb the coat every day until all the loose coat is shed out. Now, a

*Pekingese who are actively pursuing show titles need even more grooming attention and care in order to keep their coats profuse and flowing.*

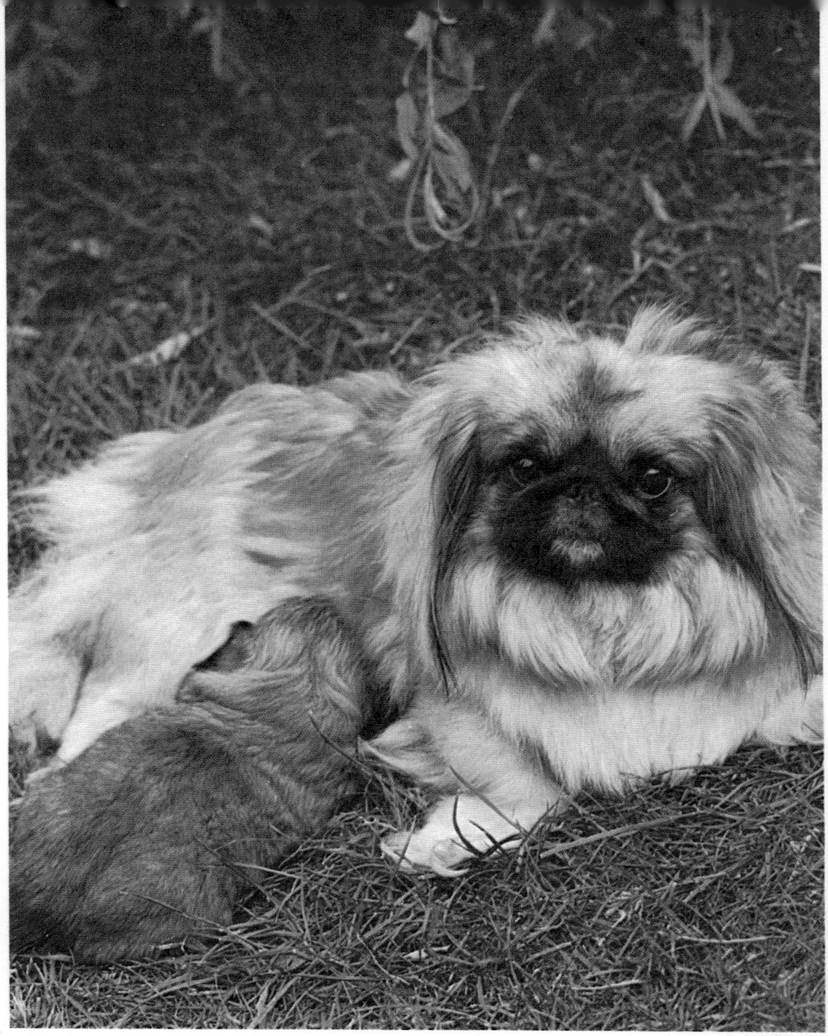

*Like the many other breeds from the Orient, the Pekingese is a patient and collected dog. Pekes make attentive and sensitive parents for their young.*

good bath will give the new coat a clean start. Brushing briskly every day will bring the new coat in glossy and healthy and much faster.

If your pet has been ill or, if a bitch is in season, and you don't want to dampen the coat for fear of chilling, a dusting with talcum powder and a good brushing will clean your pet nicely.

Remember: if a Peke is not brushed every day, there will be tangles in the coat. A well-groomed pet is a happy pet!

# Tribute to Wonderful Pekes

When a family decides to buy a house pet and the mother and children decide they would like a little Pekingese, the man of the house goes along to help select it, but often under protest. The puppy is selected to the great joy of the mother and children, but father has an expression on his face that says, "If you must have one of those silly little things, I will pay for it but don't expect me to like it." If you could drop in on the family of a new pet a week or so later, you would find that the puppy has taken complete possession of father. He was the first to suggest to mother that the puppy would be happier if his little bed were moved to their bedroom at night. He is the one who sits in the easy chair with the puppy sleeping on his lap while he reads the evening paper or watches television. He is the one down on his hands and knees rolling a ball for the puppy. And who is the first one to spoil the pup at the dinner table by sneaking him tidbits when he sits up or speaks? And when the puppy is trained to a leash, guess who takes him for his walk? Father! When he is old enough, father is the first one to suggest that he should be entered at a dog show. Why? Because there is no other dog that can compare with

*After placing Best in Show, Am. Ch. Dan Lee Dragonseed proudly sits in her trophy to pose for this photo. Owner, John Brown.*

him. The "silly thing" is now the smartest, most beautiful little dog in the world. At least the father obviously thinks so!

As an example of the Pekes' wonderful devotion, a bedridden little girl was given a Pekingese puppy after her mother had tried everything to keep up her morale and make her happy. The little girl had previously been very active and soon tired of dolls, games and other toys. The doctor suggested a pet, and after a family conference, it was decided a Pekingese puppy would be best. A little bitch puppy was selected, one that was more reserved and quieter than the other puppies in the litter; she was brought home and given to the little girl. That day was the turning point in this little girl's life. She never tired of watching the cute antics of her friend, and when she became tired, the puppy was willing to be cuddled close to her mistress and nap when she did. The little girl ate her meals eagerly now, for the puppy was fed at the same times each day in a dish by the bed with milk between meals. No more coaxing or worry for the mother, a much happier little girl, and a very, very happy puppy.

The little lion dogs are rather

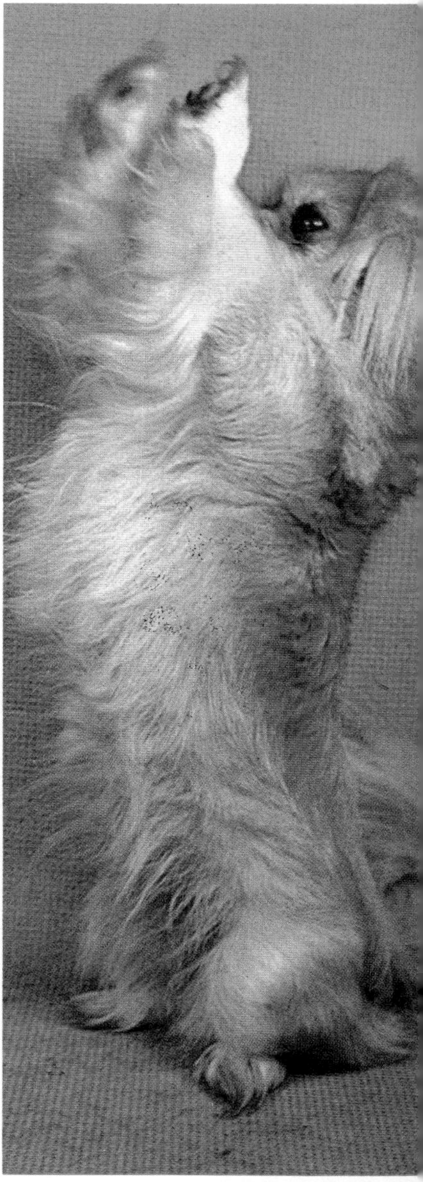

*Three cheers for wonderful Pekes! A breed as intelligent and obedient as it is charming and delightful.*

jealous by nature, or maybe possessive would be a better word. Once they take over a master and mistress, they are reluctant to share them unless they are taught to do so.

An English war bride came to America with her husband to live. In England she had lived with her mother, and they had raised Pekingese. She was unable to bring one of her pets with her, and after several months in this new, strange land she became very lonesome for her Pekingese. She decided, then, to buy one here. After visits to many kennels, she finally found a bitch that was very tiny and the type she liked. To the young bride, having this Pekingese was almost like having a baby in the home, and the young couple loved her very much. When she was almost four years old, a new baby—a "real" one—arrived in the family. Shortly after the mother came home from the hospital with the baby, she noticed her pet acting strangely: she didn't eat well and hid away in dark corners. The mother, being very busy with the new baby,

*Although some Pekes are very independent and seemingly aloof, most are affectionate and loving. Their whimsical and lighthearted way about them make them especially popular with children—these gentle and warm little gentlemen can also be quite an armful of fury and fun!*

*Whether snoozing in the emperor's silk sleeve or stowing away in their master's suitcase, Pekes—plaid and simple—love to be with their human companions.*

didn't pay too much attention to her Pekingese until she absolutely refused to eat anything at all and wouldn't even come out of her bed to greet them in the mornings. They became alarmed and took her to their veterinarian; after an examination and many questions he told them their pet was starving from lack of enough food, but also from lack of love and attention. He told them to take her home and try to give her the same attention they had given her before the new baby arrived. The first thing in the morning, they would pick her up, pet her, and make quite a fuss over her. They would feed her by hand, and soon she was eating as usual. They were very careful not to let her see them make a fuss over the baby unless one of them made a fuss over her at the same time. After a short time she was gaining weight and getting back her usual pep and personality. In a very few weeks she had made up her mind that the baby was one of her possessions too, and she was no longer jealous. When the baby was old enough to be put in a play pen, the little Pekingese was her constant guard. They are the greatest of pals, and the baby and the little pet are very happy together.

## A SPECIAL "OBEDIENCE" PEKE

The Pekingese are obedient dogs and do well in obedience trials. At an obedience trial where a Pekingese was trying to complete his Companion Dog Championship, there was a very interesting episode. This little toy dog had gone through the trial with a very good score, and the final test of the long "down" was ready to start. He followed his master and trainer up the ring and his master turned and stopped; the Peke crossed in back of him and sat down at his side, all in the proper procedure. Then the "down" signal was given and the "stay," and his master proceeded back to the other end of the ring and stood facing his little pal for the timing of the "down." There were a number of other dogs in this trial, and some were of the larger breeds; right next to the little Pekingese was a large German Shepherd Dog. Everything was very quiet and the dogs were going through their final test perfectly. The spectators were very quiet, for everyone wanted to see them all finish with good scores. With less than a minute to go, the German Shepherd Dog started working his way forward on his stomach inch by inch. He would proceed a way, then he would stop, and then go forward again. The little Peke, never moving out of position, was intently watching this procedure.

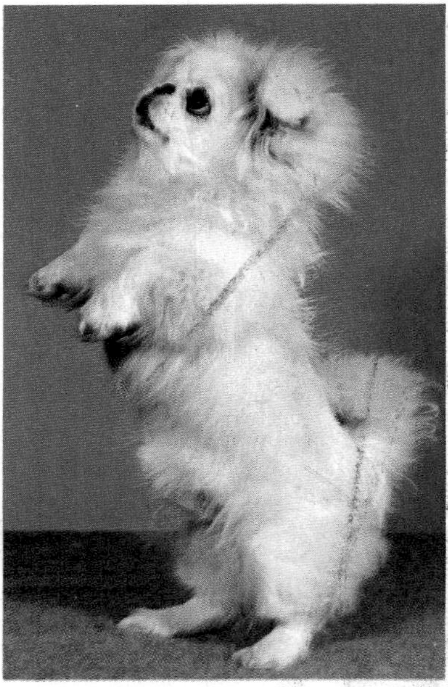

*With a face as irresistible as this one, it shouldn't take much begging to get what he wants.*

*Pekingese have done quite well in obedience trials. This Peke is being taught to broad jump.*

Glancing at his master, he wagged his tail as if he was trying to ask permission to do as the other dog. All of a sudden the German Shepherd Dog jumped to his feet and dashed toward his master. With pleading eyes and wagging tail, but still in the proper down position, the little guy watched his master. Everyone now was watching the little Peke, for no one wanted to see him make a move and spoil his chances. Still, with pleading eyes and wagging tail and now a faint whine, he begged to come to his master, but there was no signal; he knew he must not move. Everyone there must have been saying a prayer for him; it was so quiet you could have heard a pin drop. The final time was up; the signal was given by the judge; the Peke had kept his position all the time and finished in the proper form with a very good score. The applause from the crowd was deafening, and the trainer could not have been any happier than the spectators at seeing this tiny toy stay, while a larger breed walked to his master. At six months of age this Peke was trained so well that his master

*The doleful and guiltless look in this Peke's eyes certainly arouses one's curiosity as to the quality of such effortless innocence.*

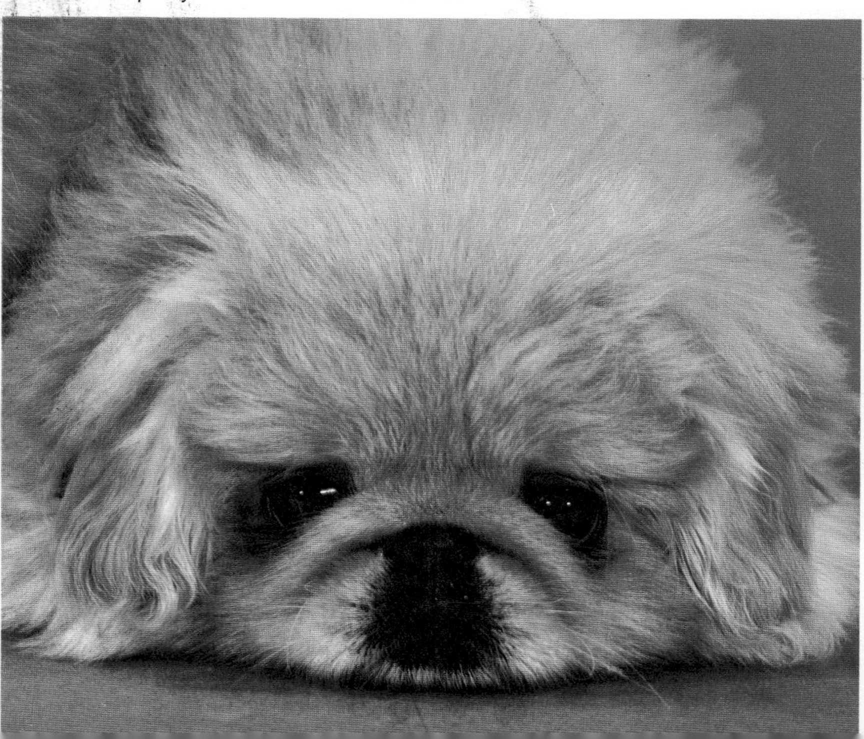

could take him to town and tell him to "stay" by the entrance to a store. He could be gone a half hour or more, and when he returned the puppy would still be sitting in the same position.

## OTHER MEMORABLE PEKES

A Pekingese bitch had a litter of puppies that she was very proud of. She would dash out of the bedroom where her little brood lived whenever she heard the doorbell, greeting the visitors as soon as the door was opened. Then she would run toward the bedroom, all the time wagging her tail and coaxing the folks to follow her. When the visitors came into the bedroom and showed their pleasure at seeing her lovely family, she would stand by, actually beaming with pride.

The owner of a lovely show Pekingese was unable to take him to an out-of-town show, so she had a friend take him. While at the show, the friend wanted to take this little fellow outside to exercise. Instead of going to his grooming case and getting the leash he was

*No longer enthroned on the pedestals of the imperial palace, the Pekingese desires only to provide his master with companionship and undying loyalty.*

used to, she had the one that belonged to her own Peke handy and decided to use it. Each time she tried to slip this leash over the head of this Peke, he would growl and snap at her; when she decided to get his own leash, he barked, wagged his tail, and practically pushed his head into the loop.

In a home where the baby was just old enough to play in a play pen with his toys, another Peke was taught to play with certain toys and never to touch the ones that belonged to the baby. He would even carry his toys into the play pen with the baby, but never carried or touched the ones that didn't belong to him.

It is easy to understand why this tiny oriental dog was the sacred dog of China, and why he is one of the most popular dogs in the world.

*Do not underestimate the intelligence of your Pekingese friend. He will know when it is time to go out and will do his best to remind an absent-minded master. Whether your dog is leashed or fenced in, it is always advisable to keep an eye on him while he is outdoors.*

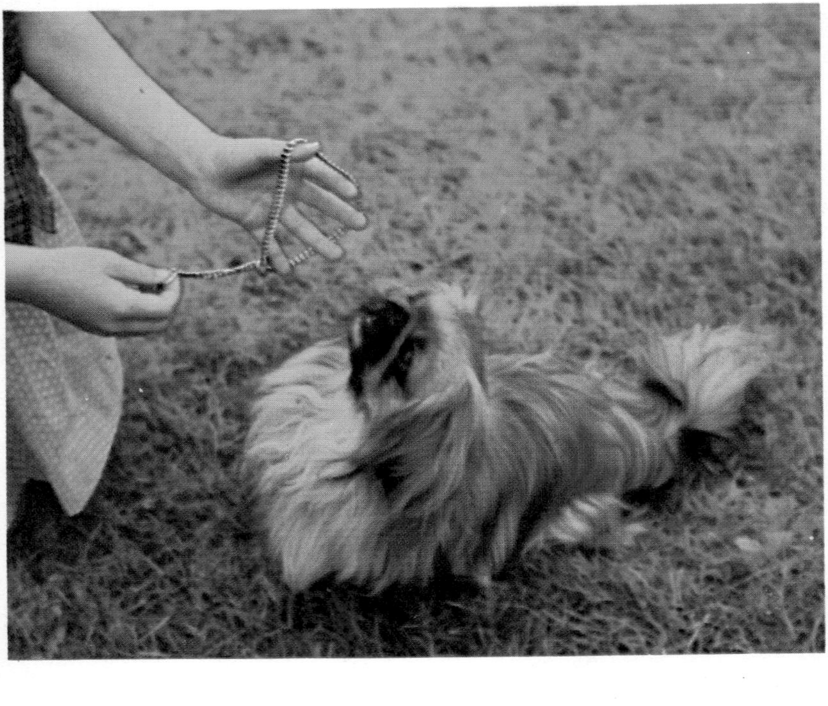

# Selecting Your Dog

Now that you have decided which dog breed suits your needs, your lifestyle, and your own temperament, there will be much to consider before you make your final purchase. Buying a puppy on impulse may only cause heartbreak later on; it makes better sense to put some real thought into your canine investment, especially since it is likely that he will share many happy years with you. Which individual will you choose as your adoring companion? Ask yourself some questions as you analyze your needs and preferences for a dog, read all that you can about your particular breed, and visit as many dog shows as possible. At the shows you will be surrounded by people who can give you all the details about the breed you are interested in buying. Decide if you want a household pet, a dog for breeding, or a show dog. Would you prefer a male or female? Puppy or adult?

If you buy from a breeder, ask him to help you with your decision. When you have settled on the dog you want, discuss with him the dog's temperament, the animal's positive and negative aspects, any health problems it might have, its feeding and grooming requirements, and whether the dog has been immunized. Reputable breeders will be willing to answer any questions you might have that pertain to the dog you have selected, and often they will make themselves available if you call for advice or if you encounter problems after you've made your purchase.

*Energetic and friendly, the Pekingese will stand on his hind legs to please you! He is very happy to please his master.*

A bit too big?
A little **too** small.
Too fuzzy for me!
Too fat to crawl.

Before you wrap it tight
And crate it home,
Behold its appetite
And room to roam.

A sloppy yap, a barking slur,
Puppy eyes to be let free,
A him? a her? an unmarked cur,
Let's pout to see its pedigree.

The perfect pet quest:
Which pup for me is best?

ANDREW DE PRISCO

Most breeders and sellers want to see their dogs placed in loving, responsible homes; they are careful about who buys their animals. So as the dog's new owner, prepare yourself for some interrogation from the breeder.

Buying a puppy should not be an impulsive endeavor; it is never wise to rush out and buy just any puppy that catches your shopping eye. The more time and thought you invest, the greater your satisfaction with your new companion. And if this new companion is to be purely a pet, its background and early care will affect its future health and good temperament. It is always essential that you choose a properly raised puppy from healthy, well-bred stock.

*This English-bred Peke is High Foo March Morning. The candid and vulnerable expression of the breed makes it most irresistible.*

You must seek out an active, sturdy puppy with bright eyes and an intelligent expression. If the puppy is friendly, that's a major plus, but you don't want one that is hyperactive nor do you want one that is dull and listless. The coat should be clean and plush, with no signs of fleas or other parasites. The premises should be clean, by sight and smell, and the proprietors should be helpful and knowledgeable. A reputable seller wants his customers satisfied and will therefore represent the puppy fairly. Let good common sense guide your purchase, and choose a reliable, well-recommended source that you know has well-satisfied customers. Don't look for a bargain, since you may end up paying many times over in future veterinarian bills, not to mention disappointments and heartache if your pet turns out not to be well. If you feel that something is lacking in the care or condition of the dogs, it is better to look elsewhere than to buy hastily and regret it afterward. Buy a healthy dog with a good disposition, one that has been

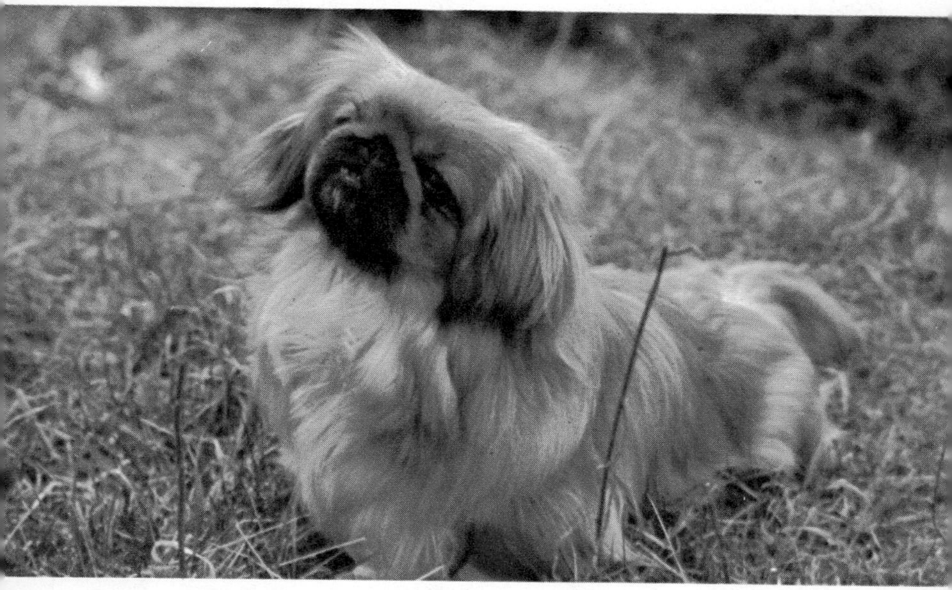

*Pekingese, when given the opportunity to be outdoors, will frolic and romp about on the lawn. Size does not necessarily dictate the amount of exercise a dog may need. An energetic Peke is a fair indicator of that.*

properly socialized and likes being around people.

If you cannot find the dog you want locally, write to the secretary of the national breed club or kennel club and ask for names of breeders near you or to whom you can write for information. Puppies are often shipped, sight unseen, from reputable breeders. In these instances, pictures and pedigree information are usually sent beforehand to help you decide. Breeders can supply you with further details and helpful guidance, if you require it. Many breed clubs provide a puppy referral service, so you may want to look into this before making your final decision.

## PET OR SHOW DOG

Conscientious breeders strive to maintain those desirable qualities in their breed. At the same time, they are always working to improve on what they have already achieved, and they do this by referring to the breed standard of perfection. The standard describes the ideal dog, and those animals that come close to the ideal are generally selected as show

*Owners of purebred dogs too often forget that all breeds of dog are interrelated. The ancient canine that is the believed ancestor of all dogs is known as Tomarctus. As packs traveled and inhabited various lands, types evolved through the process of adaptation. Later, as dogs and man joined forces, type became further diversified. This chart sketches one commonly accepted theory of the domesticated dog's development. Where does your dog fit in? With a few exceptions, dogs evolve or change as a result of a specific functional need.*

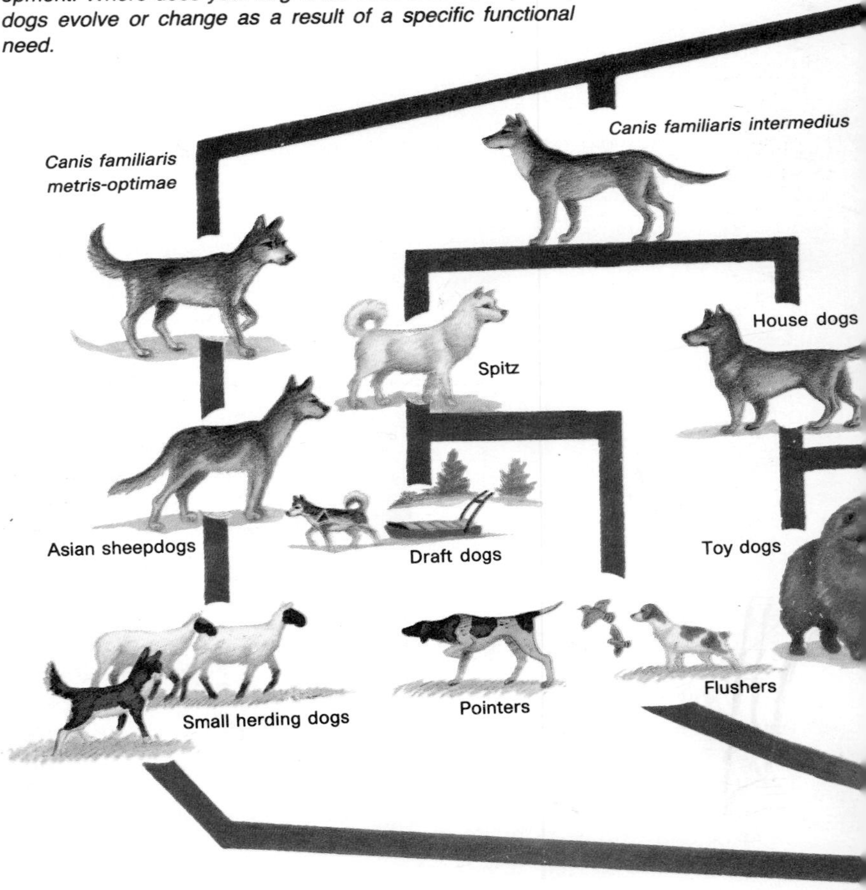

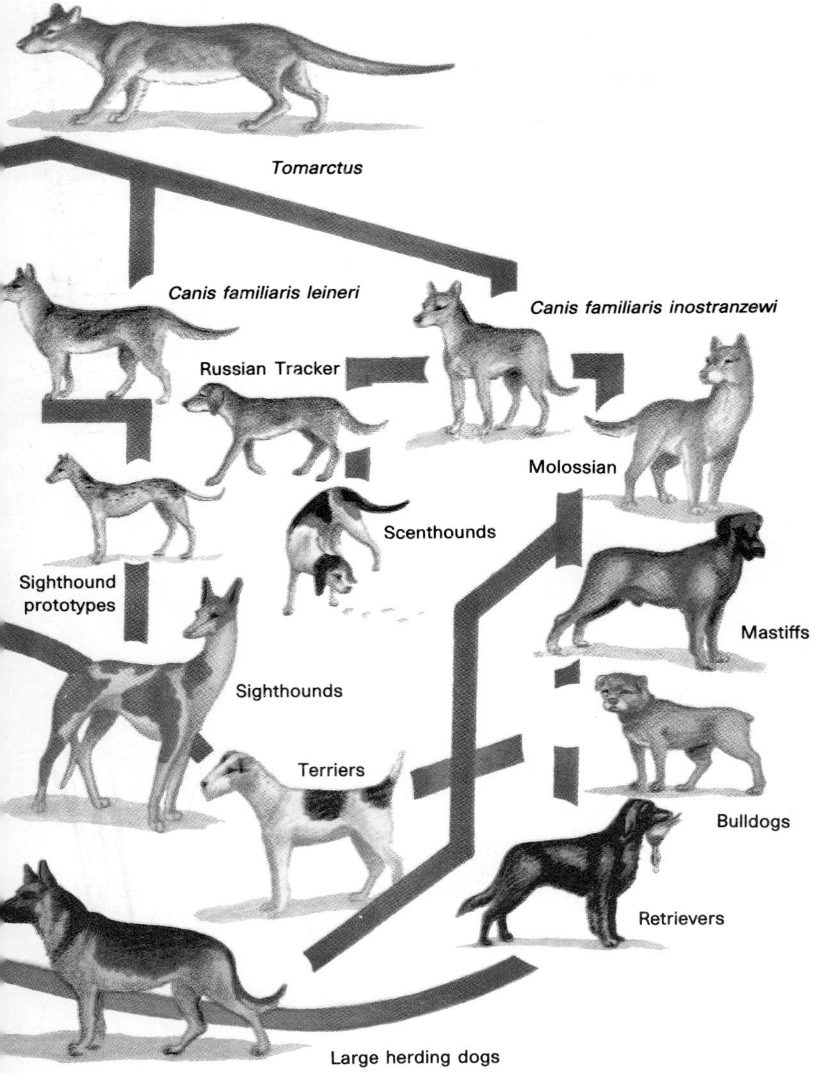

*Tomarctus*
*Canis familiaris leineri*
*Canis familiaris inostranzewi*
Russian Tracker
Molossian
Scenthounds
Sighthound prototypes
Mastiffs
Sighthounds
Terriers
Bulldogs
Retrievers
Large herding dogs

stock; those that do not are culled and sold as pets. Keep in mind that pet-quality purebred dogs are in no way less healthy or attractive than show-quality specimens. It's just that the pet may have undesirable features (such as ears that are too large or eyes that are the wrong color for its breed) which would be faults in the show ring. Often these so-called "flaws" are detectable only by experienced breeders or show judges. Naturally the more perfect animal, in terms of its breed standard, will cost more—even though he seems almost identical to his pet-quality littermate.

If you think you may eventually want to show your dog or raise a litter of puppies, by all means buy the best you can afford. You will save expense and disappointment later on. However, if the puppy is strictly to be a pet for the children, or a companion for you, you can afford to look for a bargain. The pup which is not show material, or the older pup for which there is often less demand, or the grown dog which is not being used for breeding are occasionally available and offer opportunities to save money. Remember that your initial investment may be a bargain, but it takes good food and care—and plenty of both—to raise a healthy, vigorous puppy through its adulthood.

*A proud Peke sits amid his laurels on his master 's favorite chair. Dogs who have shined in the show ring make very loving and gracious home companions as well.*

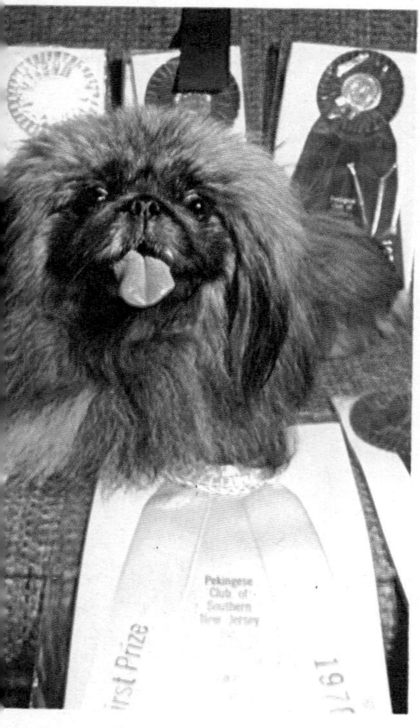

**Facing page:** *The desired coat of the Pekingese is long, straight and flat; it is well feathered with a thick undercoat. This judge at the 1987 Westmin ster Dog Show observes a competing Peke.*

The price you pay for your dog is little compared to the love and devotion he will return over the many years he'll be with you. With proper care and affection, your pup should live to a ripe old age; thanks to modern veterinary science and improvements in canine nutrition, dogs today are better maintained and live longer. It is not uncommon to see dogs living well into their teens.

Generally speaking, small dogs live longer than big ones. With love and the proper care any dog will live to its optimum age. Many persons, however, opt for a particular breed because of its proven longevity. This, of course, is purely a personal decision.

## MALE OR FEMALE

Let us first disregard the usual generalizations and misconceptions applied to male vs. female dogs and consider the practical concerns. If you intend to show your new dog, a male will likely closer adhere to the

*Size variation in the dog family is extreme. The consideration of size must be a high priority when choosing a breed. The amount of housing, exercise, and food required, as well as the animal's lifespan are just some of the factors involved.*

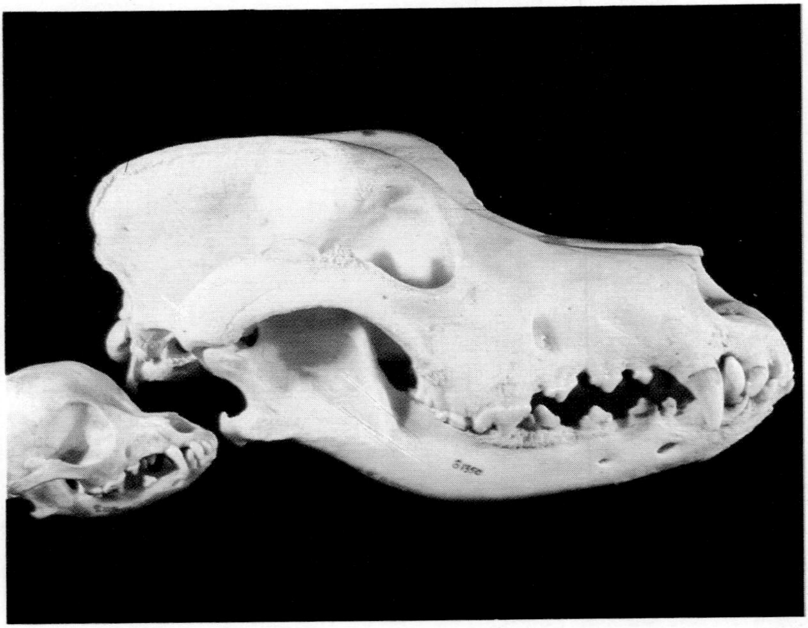

breed standard, though ring competition for males is stiffer. A female chosen to show cannot be spayed and the owner must contend with the bitch's heat period. If it is solely a pet—and pet animals should *not* be bred—castration or spaying is necessary. Neutered pets have longer lifespans and have a decreased risk of cancer. Males are more economical to neuter than are females. You might also consider that females are generally smaller than males, easier to housetrain, may be more family-oriented and protective of home and property. Any dog will roam—male or female—castration will not affect roaming in most cases. Males are larger and stronger, proving better guard-dog candidates. Of course, a dog of either sex, if properly trained, can make a charming, reliable, and loving pet. Male vs. female is chiefly a matter of personal preference—go with your first instinct.

## ADULT OR PUP

Whether to buy a grown dog or a young puppy is another question. It is surely an undeniable pleasure to watch your dog grow from a lively pup to a mature, dignified dog. If you don't have the time to spend on the more frequent meals, housebreaking, and other training a puppy needs in order to become a dog you can be

**Life Expectancy**

| *Dog's Age in Years* | *Comparative Human Age in Years* |
|---|---|
| 1 | ......15 |
| 2 | ......24 |
| 3 | ......28 |
| 4 | ......32 |
| 5 | ......36 |
| 6 | ......40 |
| 7 | ......44 |
| 8 | ......48 |
| 9 | ......52 |
| 10 | ......56 |
| 11 | ......60 |
| 12 | ......64 |
| 13 | ......68 |
| 14 | ......72 |
| 15 | ......76 |
| 16 | ......80 |
| 17 | ......84 |
| 18 | ......88 |
| 19 | ......92 |
| 20 | ......96 |
| 21 | ......100 |

*This chart is designed to provide a comparative view of ages between a dog and its human counterpart. Necessarily it is an oversimplification since larger breeds often have shorter lifespans than do average or medium-sized dogs; likewise working dogs may tend to live shorter lives than the easy-going pet dog. These factors, and many others, must be taken into account when considering this chart.*

proud of, then choose an older, partly-trained adolescent or a grown dog. If you want a show dog, remember that no one, not even an expert, can predict with one hundred percent accuracy what a puppy will be like when he grows up. The dog may seem to exhibit show potential *most* of the time, but six months is the earliest age for the would-be exhibitor to select a prospect and know that its future is in the show ring.

If you have a small child, it is best to get a puppy big enough to defend itself, one not less than four or five months old. Older children will enjoy playing with and helping to take care of a baby pup; but at less than four months, a puppy wants to do little else but eat and sleep, and he must be protected from teasing and overtiring. You cannot expect a very young child to understand that a puppy is a fragile living being; to the youngster he is a toy like his

*One of the breed's most cherished characteristics is its eyes—deep and expressive and never compromising the breed's age-old dignity and nobility.*

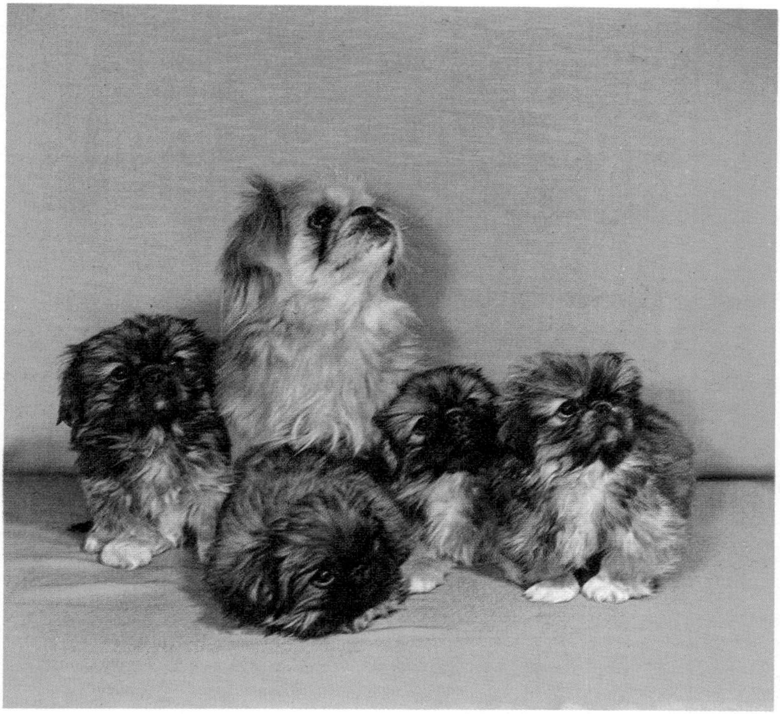

*Selecting a pup from a litter as charming as this one would certainly be difficult.*

stuffed dog. Children, therefore, must learn how to handle and care for their young pets.

We recommend you start with a puppy so that you can raise and train it according to the rules you have established in your own home. While a dog is young, its behavior can be more easily shaped by the owner, whereas an older dog , although trainable, may be a bit set in his ways.

## WHAT TO LOOK FOR IN A PUPPY

In choosing a puppy, assuming that it comes from healthy, well-bred parents, look for one that is friendly and outgoing. The biggest pup in the litter is apt to be somewhat coarse as a grown dog, while the appealing "runt of the litter" may turn out to be a timid shadow—or have a Napoleonic complex! If you want a show dog and have no experience in choosing a prospect, study the breed standard and listen carefully to the breeder on the finer points of show conformation. A breeder's prices will be in accord with his puppies' expected worth, and he will be honest with you about each pup's potential because it is to his own advantage. He wants his top-quality show puppies placed in the public eye to reflect glory on him—and to attract future buyers. Why should he sell a potential show champion to someone who just wants a pet?

Now that you have paid your money and made your choice, you are ready to depart with puppy, papers, and instructions. Make sure that you know the youngster's feeding routine, and take along some of his food. For the trip home, place him in a comfortable, sturdy carrier. Do not drive home with a puppy on your lap! If you'll be travelling for a few hours, at the very least bring along a bottle of water from the breeder and a small water dish.

## PEDIGREE AND REGISTRATION

Owners of puppies are often misled by sellers with such ruses as leading the owner to believe his dog is something special. The term *pedigree papers* is quite different from the term *registration papers.* A pedigree is nothing more than a statement made by the breeder of the dog;

*If you have never been to a dog show, whether you're interested in show dogs or not, by all means—Go! An all-breed dog show will give you hands-on experience with different breeds of dog, the chance to meet their owners and breeders, and the answers to many of your questions.*

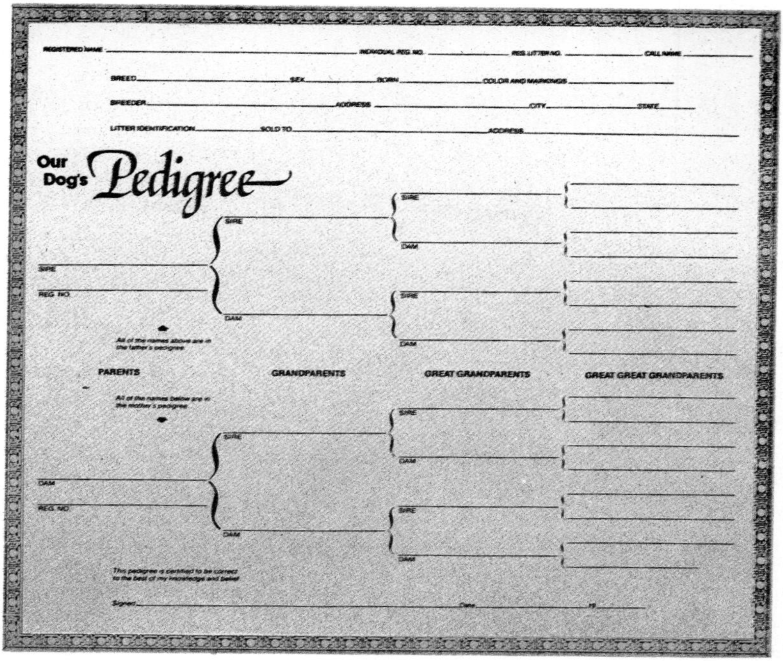


*Pedigree papers can trace a dog's lineage back several generations. They do not, however, guarantee that a puppy is purebred, healthy or sound.*

and it is written on special pedigree blanks, which are readily available from any pet shop or breed club, with the names of several generations from which the new puppy comes. It records your puppy's ancestry and other important data, such as the pup's date of birth, its breed, its sex, its sire and dam, its breeder's name and address, and so on. If your dog has had purebred champions in his background, then the pedigree papers are valuable as evidence of the good breeding behind your dog; but if the names on the pedigree paper are meaningless, then so is the paper itself. Just because a dog has a pedigree doesn't necessarily mean he is registered with a kennel club.

Registration papers from the American Kennel Club or the United Kennel Club in the United States or The Kennel Club of Great Britain attest to the fact that the mother and father of your puppy were purebred dogs of the breed represented by your puppy and that they were registered with a particular club. Normally every registered dog also has a complete pedigree available. Registration papers, which you receive when you buy a puppy, merely enable you to register your puppy. Usually the breeder has registered only the litter, so it is the new owner's responsibility to register and name an individual pup. The papers should be filled out and sent to the appropriate address printed on the application, along with the fee required for the registration. A certificate of registration will then be sent to you.

Pedigree and registration, by the way, have nothing to do with licensing, which is a local regulation applying to purebred and mongrel alike. Find out what the local ordinance is in your town or city and how it applies to your dog; then buy a license and keep it on your dog's collar for identification.

*Whether you are choosing a pet- or show-quality Peke, you can be assured that he will be a delight to own.*

# The New Family Member

*Every Peke has a personality most certainly his own and will share this uniqueness and specialness with his new family.*

At long last, the day you have all been waiting for, your new puppy will make its grand entrance into your home. Before you bring your companion to its new residence, however, you must plan carefully for its arrival. Keep in mind that the puppy will need time to adjust to life with a different owner. He may seem a bit apprehensive about the strange surroundings in which he finds himself, having spent the first few weeks of life with his dam and littermates, but in a couple of days, with love and patience on your part, the transition will be complete.

First impressions are important, especially from the puppy's point of view, and these may very well set the pattern of his future relationship with you. You must be consistent in the way you handle your pet so that he learns what is expected of him. He must come to trust and respect you as his keeper and master. Provide him with proper care and attention, and you will be rewarded with a loyal companion for many years. Considering the needs of your puppy and planning ahead will surely make the change from his former home to his new one easier.

## ADVANCE PREPARATION

In preparing for your puppy's arrival, perhaps more important than anything else is to find out from the seller how the pup was maintained. What brand of food was offered and when and how often was the puppy fed? Has

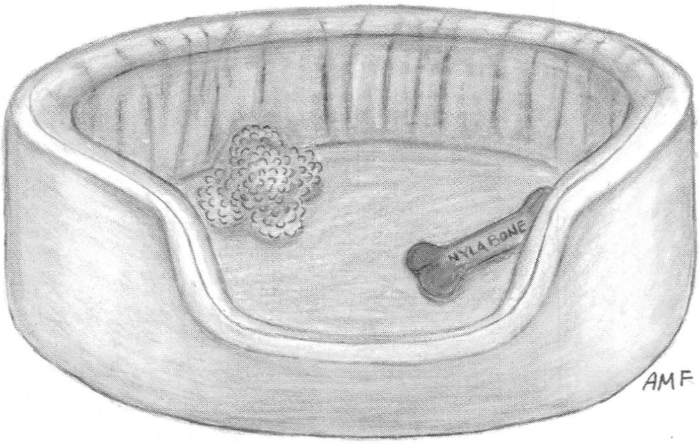


*The puppy's bed will provide a place of refuge and privacy. Make sure that the puppy's toilet needs have been met before sending him to bed for the night.*

## BASIC PUPPY NEEDS

- Canned and dry food/diet schedule
- Feeding and water bowls
- Carrying/sleeping crate
- Bed
- Collar and leash
- Grooming supplies (brushes, shampoo, etc.)
- Outdoor lead and/or pen
- Muzzle/first-aid kit
- Flea collar and preparations
- Safe chew products (Nylabone®, Gumabone®)
- Edible chew products (treats/rewards)

*This chart lists some of the many items that the dog owner should have on hand before he brings home his new charge.*

the pup been housebroken; if so, what method was employed? Attempt to continue whatever routine was started by the person from whom you bought your puppy; then, gradually, you can make those changes that suit you and your lifestyle. If, for example, the puppy has been paper trained, plan to stock up on newspaper. Place this newspaper toilet facility in a selected spot so that your puppy learns to use the designated area as his "bathroom." And keep on hand a supply of the dog food to which he is accustomed, as a sudden switch to new food could cause digestive upsets.

Another consideration is sleeping and resting quarters. Be sure to supply a dog bed for your pup, and introduce him to his special cozy corner so that he knows where to retire when he feels like taking a snooze. You'll need to buy a collar (or harness) and leash, a safe chew item (such as Nylabone® or Gumabone®), and a few grooming tools as well. A couple of sturdy feeding dishes, one for food and one for water, will be needed; and it will be necessary, beforehand, to set up a feeding station.

### FINDING A VETERINARIAN

An important part of your preparations should include finding a local veterinarian who can provide quality health care in the form of routine check-ups, inoculations, and prompt medical attention in case of illness or an emergency. Find out if the animal you have selected has been vaccinated against canine diseases, and make certain you secure all health certificates at the time of purchase. This information will be valuable to your veterinarian, who will want to know the puppy's complete medical history. Incidentally, don't wait until your puppy becomes sick before you seek the services of a vet; make an appointment for your pup before or soon after he takes up residence with you so that he starts out with a clean bill of health in his new home.

**CHILDREN AND PUPPIES**

Prepare the young members of the household on pet care. Children should learn not only to love their charges but to respect them and treat them with the consideration one would give all living things. It must be emphasized to youngsters that the puppy has certain needs, just as humans have, and all family members must take an active role in ensuring that these needs are met. Someone must feed the puppy. Someone must walk him a couple of times a day or clean up after him if he is trained to relieve himself on newspaper. Someone must groom his coat, clean his ears, and clip his nails from time to time. Someone must see to it that the puppy gets sufficient exercise and attention each day.

A child who has a pet to care for learns responsibility; nonetheless, parental guidance is an essential part of his learning experience. Many a child has been known to "love a pet to death," squeezing and hugging the animal in ways which are irritating or even painful. Others have been found guilty of teasing, perhaps unintentionally, and disturbing their pet while the animal is eating or resting. One must teach a child, therefore, when and how to gently stroke and fondle a puppy. In time, the child can learn how to carefully pick up and handle the pup. A dog should always be supported with both hands, *not* lifted by the scruff of the neck. One hand placed under the chest, between the front legs, and the other hand supporting the dog's rear end will be comfortable and will restrain the animal as you hold and carry him. Always demonstrate to children the proper way to lift a dog.

**BE A GOOD NEIGHBOR**

For the sake of your dog's safety and well being, don't allow him to wander onto the property of others. Keep him confined at all times to your own yard or indoors where he won't become a nuisance. Consider what

*As adorable and lovable as they are haughty and bold, the Pekingese have fascinated dog lovers for centuries. Owner, Shirley Schwartz.*

Clockwise from upper right: *pokeweed, jimson weed, foxglove, and yew. If ingested, any toxic plant can be dangerous to your dog.*

*Dog theft is not an uncommon event. Dognappers will steal either a purebred or mongrel puppy so all owners must always be wary.*

dangers lie ahead for an unleashed dog that has total freedom of the great outdoors, particularly when he is unsupervised by his master. There are cars and trucks to dodge on the streets and highways. There are stray animals with which to wrangle. There are poisons all around, such as car antifreeze in driveways or toxic plants and shrubs, which, if swallowed, could prove fatal. There are dognappers and sadistic people who may steal or bring harm to your beloved pet. In short, there are all sorts of nasty things waiting to hurt him. Did you know that if your dog consumes rotting garbage, there is the possibility he could go into shock or even die? And are you aware that a dog left to roam in a wooded area or field could become infected with any number of parasites if he plays with or ingests some small prey, such as a rabbit, that might be carrying these parasitic organisms? A thorn from a rosebush imbedded in the dog's foot pad, tar from a newly paved road stuck to his coat, and a wound inflicted by a wild animal all can be avoided if you take the precaution of keeping your dog in a safe enclosure where he will be protected from such dangers. Don't let your dog run loose; he is likely to stray from home and get into all sorts of trouble.

### GETTING ACQUAINTED

Plan to bring your new pet home in the morning so that by nightfall he will have had some time to become acquainted with you and his new environment. Avoid introducing the pup to the family around holiday time, since all of the extra excitement will only add to the confusion and frighten him. Let the puppy enter your home on a day when the routine is normal. For those people who work during the week, a Saturday morning is an ideal time to bring the puppy to his new home; this way he has the entire weekend to make adjustments before being left alone for a few hours, come Monday morning.

Let the puppy explore, under your watchful eye of course, and let him come to know his new home without stress and fear. Resist the temptation to handle him too much during these first few days. And, if there are other dogs or animals around the house, make certain all are properly introduced. If you observe fighting among the animals, or some other problem, you may have to separate all parties until they learn to accept one another. Remember that neglecting your other pets while

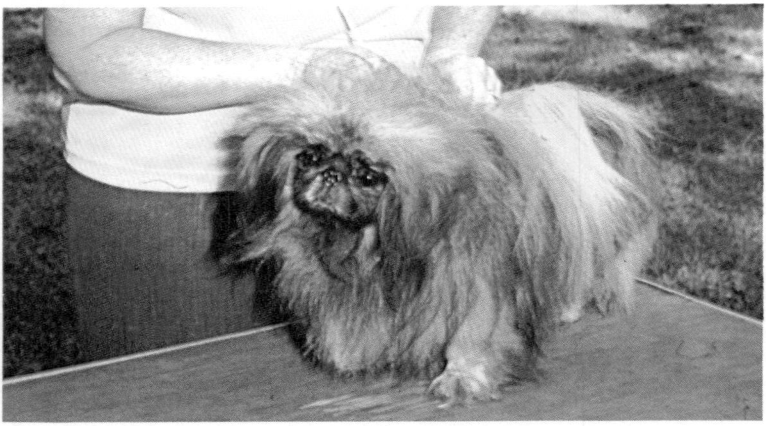

*A well-groomed Peke is a source of unabounding pride and joy to his master.*

**Facing page:** *Among the toy dogs, the Pekingese is hailed as the aristocrat—his self-confident, bold way about himself has earned him this distinction.*

showering the new puppy with extra attention will only cause animosity and jealousy. Make an effort to pay special attention to the other animals as well.

On that eventful first night, try not to give in and let the puppy sleep with you; otherwise, this could become a difficult habit to break. Let him cry and whimper, even if it means a night of restlessness for the entire family. Some people have had success with putting a doll or a hot water bottle wrapped in a towel in the puppy's bed as a surrogate mother, while others have placed a ticking alarm clock in the bed to simulate the heartbeat of the pup's dam and littermates. Remember that this furry little fellow is used to the warmth and security of his mother and siblings, so the adjustment to sleeping alone will take time. Select a location away from drafts and away from the feeding station for placement of his dog bed. Keep in mind, also, that the bed should be roomy enough for him to stretch out in; as he grows older, you may need to supply a larger one.

Prior to the pup's arrival, set up his room and partition it the way you would to keep an infant out of a particular area. You may want to keep his bed, his feeding station, and his toilet area all in the same room—in separate locations—or you may want to set the feeding station up in your kitchen, where meals for all family members are served. Whatever you decide, do it ahead of time so you will have that much less to worry about when your puppy finally moves in with you.

Above all else, be patient with your puppy as he adjusts to life in his new home. If you purchase a pup that is not housebroken, you will have to spend time with the dog—just as you would with a small child—until he develops proper toilet habits. Even a housebroken puppy may feel nervous in strange new surroundings and have an occasional accident. Praise and encouragement will elicit far better results than punishment or scolding. Remember that your puppy wants nothing more than to please you, thus he is anxious to learn the behavior that is required of him.

# Feeding Requirements

Perhaps more than any other single aspect of your dog's development, proper feeding requires an educated and responsible dog owner. The importance of nutrition on your dog's bone and muscle growth cannot be overemphasized. Soon after your puppy comes to live with you, he will need to be fed. Remember to ask the seller what foods were given to the youngster and stay with that diet for a while. It is important for the puppy to keep eating and to avoid skipping a meal, so entice him with the food to which he is accustomed. If you prefer to switch to some other brand of dog food, each day begin to add small quantities of the new brand to the usual food offering. Make the portions of the new food progressively larger until the pup is weaned from his former diet.

What should you feed the puppy and how often? His diet is really quite simple and relatively inexpensive to prepare. Puppies need to be fed small portions at frequent intervals, since they are growing and their activity level is high. You must ensure that your pup gains weight steadily; with an adult dog, however, growth slows down and weight must be regulated to prevent obesity and a host of other problems. At one time, it was thought that home-cooked meals were the answer, with daily rations of meat,

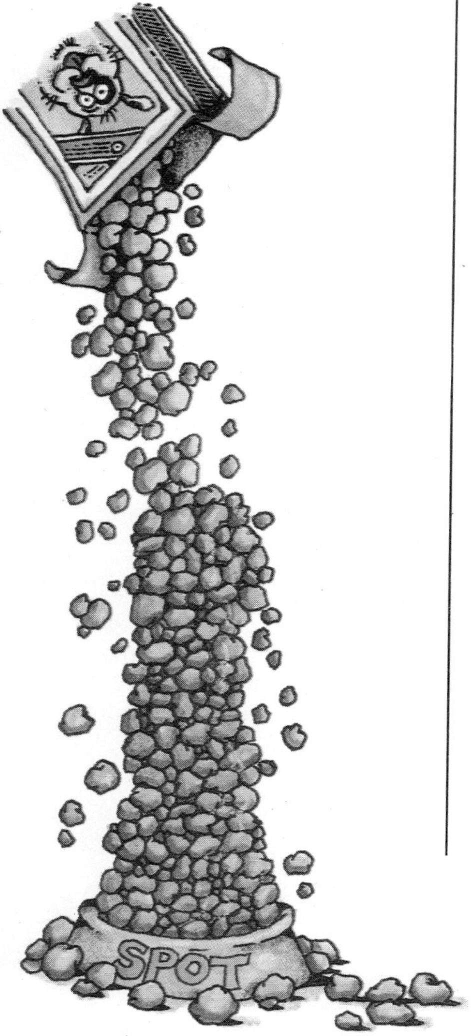


*Choosing a quality dog food from your pet shop is easy—deciding how much to feed may not be as straightforward. Feedings must always be carefully monitored.*

vegetables, egg yolk, cereal, cheese, brewer's yeast, and vitamin supplements. With all of the nutritionally complete commercial dog food products readily available, these time-consuming preparations really are unnecessary now. A great deal of money and research has resulted in foods that we can serve our dogs with confidence and pride; and most of these commercial foods have been developed along strict guidelines according to the size, weight, and age of your dog. These products are reasonably priced, easy to find, and convenient to store.

**THE PUPPY'S MEALS**

After a puppy has been fully weaned from its mother until approximately three months of age, it needs to be fed four times a day. In the morning and evening offer kibble (dog meal) soaked in hot water or broth, to which you have added some canned meat-based food or fresh raw meat cut into small chunks. At noon and bedtime feed him a bit of kibble or whole-grain cereal moistened with milk (moistening, by the way, makes the food easier to digest, since dogs don't typically chew their food). From three to six months,

*No matter what size your dog is, he will need to chew. A Nylabone® or a similar safe chew toy is highly recommended by countless vets and breeders.*

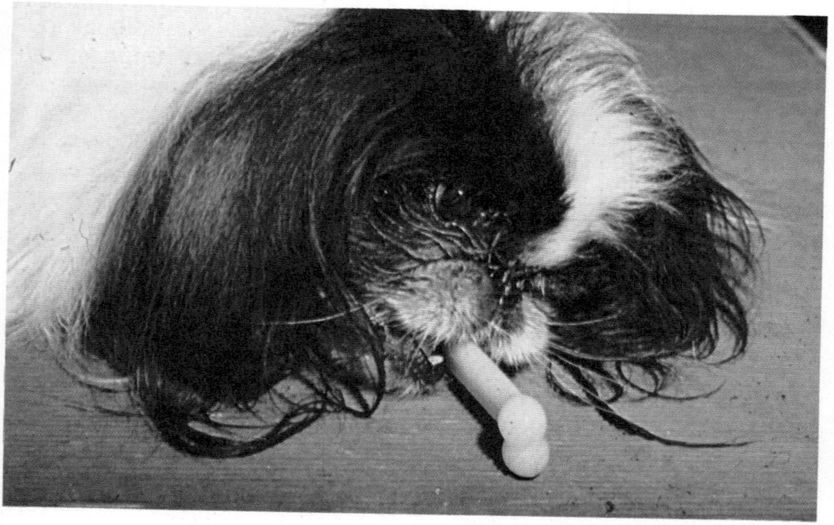

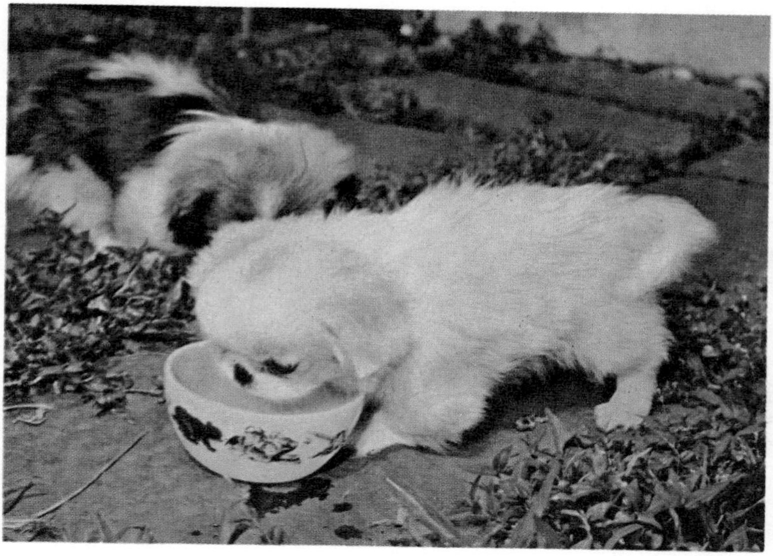

*In order for your puppy to grow up healthy and strong, intelligent feeding habits must be adhered to.*

offer just three meals—one milk and two meat. At six months, two meals are sufficient; at one year, a single meal can be given, supplemented with a few dry biscuits in the morning and evening. During the colder months, especially if your dog is active, you might want to mix in some wheat germ oil or corn oil or bacon drippings with the meal to add extra calories. Remember to keep a bowl of cool, fresh water on hand always to help your dog regulate its body temperature and to aid in digestion.

From one year on, you may continue feeding the mature dog a single meal (in the evening, perhaps, when you have your supper), or you may prefer to divide this meal in two, offering half in the morning and the other half at night. Keep in mind that while puppies require foods in small chunks, or nuggets, older dogs can handle larger pieces of food at mealtime. Discuss your dog's feeding schedule with your veterinarian; he can make suggestions about the right diet for your particular canine friend.

**COMPARISON SHOPPING**

With so many fine dog-food products on the market today, there is something for everyone's pet. You may want to serve dry food "as is" or mix it with warm water or broth. Perhaps you'll choose to combine dry food with fresh or canned preparations. Some canned foods contain all meat, but they are not complete; others are mixtures of meat and grains, which have been fortified with additional nutrients to make them more complete and balanced. There are also various packaged foods that can be served alone or as supplements and that can be left out for a few hours without spoiling. This self-feeding method, which works well for dogs that are not prone to weight problems, allows the animal to serve himself whenever he feels hungry. Many people who work during the day find these dry or semi-moist rations convenient to use, and these foods are great to bring along if you travel with your dog.

Be sure to read the labels carefully before you make your dog-food purchases. Most

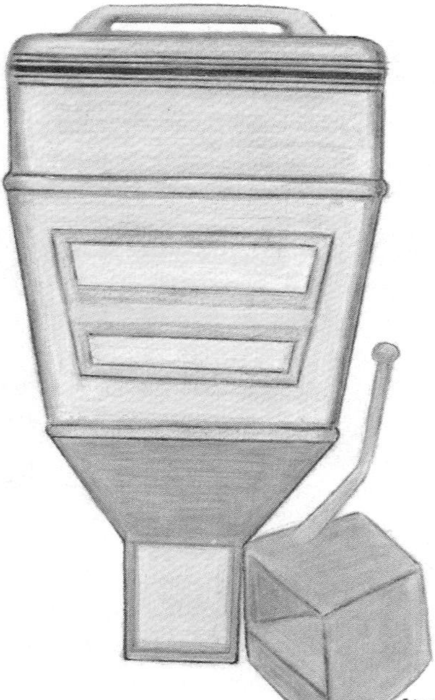


*Feeder bins are used by many kennel owners as well as pet owners. These devices help to conveniently store and distribute dry foods in a sanitary, efficient way.*

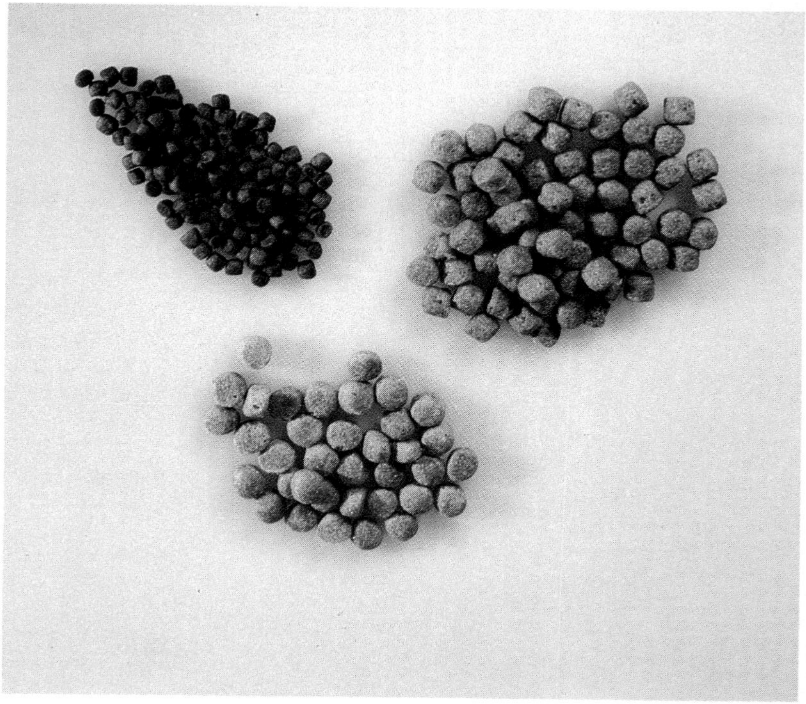

*Pet shops offer a variety of dry kibbles. Though the nutritional values of these foods are essentially equivalent, compare the manufacturer's labels.*

reputable pet-food manufacturers list the ingredients and the nutritional content right on the can or package. Instructions are usually included so that you will know how much to feed your dog to keep him thriving and in top condition. A varied, well-balanced diet that supplies the proper amounts of protein, carbohydrate, fat, vitamins, minerals, and water is important to keep your puppy healthy and to guarantee his normal development. Adjustments to the diet can be made, under your veterinarian's supervision, according to the individual puppy, his rate of growth, his activity level, and so on. Liquid or powder vitamin and mineral supplements, or those in tablet form, are available and can be given if you need to feel certain that the diet is balanced.

*Pekingese owners seem to agree that their dogs are as unpredictable and entertaining as they are loving and adorable. Pekes surely enjoy all the attention they receive from their antics and waggery.*

## DEVELOPING GOOD EATING HABITS

Try to serve your puppy his meals at the same time each day and in the same location so that he will get used to his daily routine and develop good eating habits. A bit of raw egg, cottage cheese, or table scraps (leftover food from your own meals) can be offered from time to time; but never accustom your dog to eating human "junk food." Cake, candy, chocolate, soda, and other snack foods are for people, not dogs. Besides, these foods provide only "empty" calories that your pet doesn't need if he is to stay healthy. Avoid offering spicy, fried, fatty, or starchy foods; rather, offer leftover meats, vegetables, and gravies. Get in the habit of feeding your puppy or your grown dog his *own* daily meals of dog food. If ever you are in doubt about what foods and how much to serve, consult your veterinarian.

*Four Paws Good 'N Plenty Feeder is designed to hold approximately 2 pounds of food. The Good 'N Plenty Waterer holds a generous 3 quarts. Both are designed for easy dismantling and cleaning.*

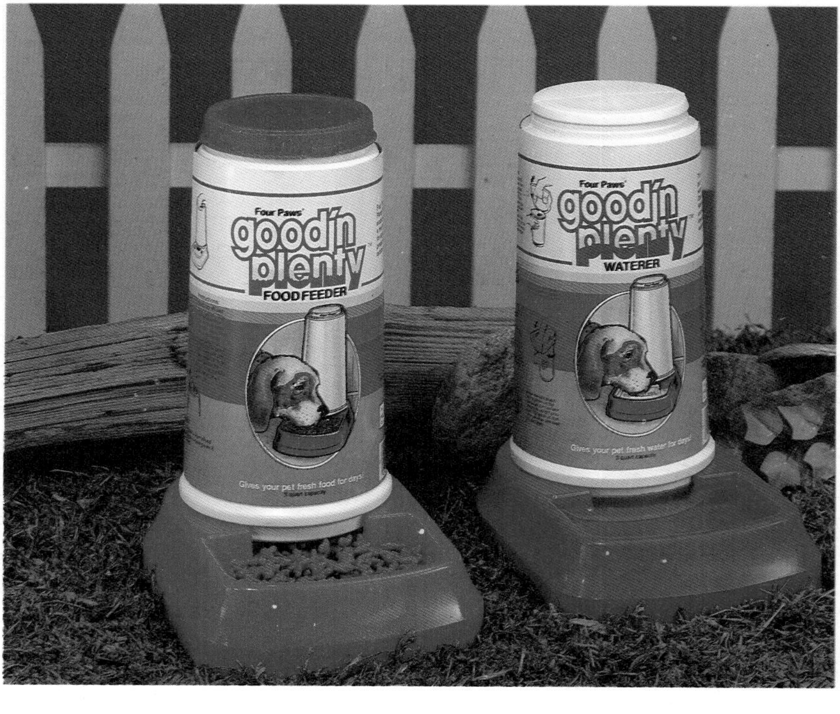

## FEEDING GUIDELINES

Some things to bear in mind with regard to your dog's feeding regimen follow.

• Nutritional balance, provided by many commercial dog foods, is vital; avoid feeding a one-sided all-meat diet. Variety in the kinds of meat (beef, lamb, chicken, liver) or cereal grains (wheat, oats, corn) that you offer your dog is of secondary importance compared to the balance or "completeness" of dietary components.

• Always refrigerate opened canned food so that it doesn't spoil. Remember to remove all uneaten portions of canned or moistened food from the feeding dish as soon as the pup has finished his meal. Discard the leftover food immediately and thoroughly wash and dry the feeding dish, as a dirty dish is a breeding ground for harmful germs.

• When offering dry foods, always keep a supply of water on hand for your dog. Water should be made available at all times, even if dry foods are not left out for self-feeding. Each

*Feeding your dog is made easy by the use of sturdy non-tip, easy-clean bowls. Pet shops offer the best selection of colors, styles and sizes.*

day the water dish should be washed with soap and hot water, rinsed well, and dried; a refill of clean, fresh water should be provided daily.

• Food and water should be served at room temperature, neither too hot nor too cold, so that it is more palatable for your puppy.

• Serve your pup's meals in sturdy hard-plastic, stainless steel, or earthenware containers, ones that won't tip over as the dog gulps his food down. Some bowls and dishes are weighted to prevent spillage, while others fit neatly into holders which offer support. Feeding dishes should be large enough to hold each meal.

• Whenever the nutritional needs of your dog change—that is to say, when it grows older or if it becomes ill, obese, or pregnant; or if it starts to nurse its young—special diets are in order. Always contact your vet for advice on these special dietary requirements.

• Feed your puppy at the same regular intervals each day; reserve treats for special occasions or, perhaps, to reward good behavior during training sessions.

• Hard foods, such as biscuits and dog meal, should be offered regularly. Chewing on these hard, dry morsels helps the dog keep its teeth clean and its gums conditioned.

• Never overfeed your dog. If given the chance, he will accept and relish every in-between-meal tidbit you offer him. This pampering will only put extra weight on your pet and cause him to be unhealthy in the long run.

• Do not encourage your dog to beg for food from the table while you are eating your meals.

• Food can be effectively used by the owner to train the dog. Doggie treats are practical and often nutritional—choose your chew treats choosily.

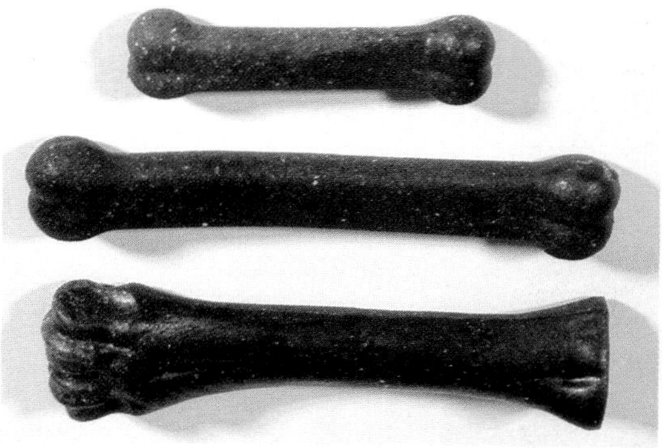

*New treats on the block by Nylabone®. These Chooz® crunchy dog bones are delectable and affordable.*

## FEEDING CHART

| Age and No. of Feedings Per Day | Weight in Lbs. | Weight in Kg. | Caloric Requirement kcal M.E./Day |
|---|---|---|---|
| **Puppies—Weaning to 3 months** Four per day | 1–3 | .5–1.4 | 124–334 |
| | 3–6 | 1.4–2.7 | 334–574 |
| | 6–12 | 2.7–5.4 | 574–943 |
| | 12–20 | 5.4–9.1 | 943–1384 |
| | 15–30 | 6.8–13.6 | 1113–1872 |
| **Puppies—3 to 6 months** Three per day | 3–10 | 1.4–4.5 | 334–816 |
| | 5–15 | 2.3–6.8 | 494–1113 |
| | 12–25 | 5.4–11.3 | 943–1645 |
| | 20–40 | 9.1–18.2 | 1384–2352 |
| | 30–70 | 13.6–31.8 | 1872–3542 |
| **Puppies—6 to 12 months** Two per day | 6–12 | 2.7–5.4 | 574–943 |
| | 12–25 | 5.4–11.3 | 943–1645 |
| | 20–50 | 9.1–22.7 | 1384–2750 |
| | 40–70 | 18.2–31.8 | 2352–3542 |
| | 70–100 | 31.8–45.4 | 3542–4640 |
| **Normally Active Adults** One or two per day | 6–12 | 2.7–5.4 | 286–472 |
| | 12–25 | 5.4–11.3 | 472–823 |
| | 25–50 | 11.3–22.7 | 823–1375 |
| | 50–90 | 22.7–40.8 | 1375–2151 |
| | 90–175 | 40.8–79.4 | 2151–3675 |

*This chart presents general parameters of the dog's caloric requirements, based on weight. The total caloric intake comes from a complete, balanced diet of quality foods. To assist owners, dog food companies generally provide the nutritional information to their product right on the label.*

## Accommodations

Puppies newly weaned from their mother and siblings should be kept warm at all times. As they get older, they can be acclimated gradually to cooler temperatures. When you purchase your dog, find out from the seller whether he is hardy and can withstand the rigors of outdoor living. Many breeds have been known to adapt well to a surprising number of environments, so long as they are given time to adjust. If your pup is to be an indoor companion, perhaps a dog bed in the corner of the family room will suffice; or you may want to invest in a crate for him to call his "home" whenever he needs to be confined for short intervals. You might plan to partition off a special room, or part of a room, for your pooch; or you may find that a heated garage or finished basement works well as your dog's living quarters. If your breed can tolerate living outside, you may want to buy or build him his own dog house with an attached run. It might be feasible to place his house in your fenced-in backyard. The breed that can live outdoors fares well when given access to some sort of warm, dry shelter during periods of inclement weather. As you begin thinking about where your canine friend will spend most of his time, you'll want to consider his breed, his age, his temperament, his need for exercise, and the money, space, and resources you have available to house him.

*A bed for your dog gives him a place to call his own. His bed should be placed in a warm, dry, draft-free area.*

## THE DOG BED

In preparing for your puppy's arrival, it is recommended that a dog bed be waiting for him so that he has a place to sleep and rest. If you have provided him with his own bed or basket, ensure that it is placed in a warm, dry, draft-free spot that is private but at the same time near the center of family activity. Refrain from placing his bed near the feed and water dishes or his toilet area. You may want to give your puppy something with which to snuggle, such as a laundered towel or blanket or an article of old clothing. Some dogs have been known to chew apart their beds and bedding, but you can easily channel this chewing energy into more constructive behavior simply by supplying him with some safe toys or a Nylabone® pacifier for gnawing. Pet shops stock dog beds, among other supplies that you might need for your pup. Select a bed that is roomy, comfortable, and easy to clean, keeping in mind that you may have to replace the smaller bed with a larger one as the puppy grows to adulthood. Remember to clean and disinfect the bed and sleeping area from time to time, as these can become parasitic playgrounds for fleas, lice, mites, and the like.

*Beds can have personality. Pet shops offer many different bedding options to the owner willing to explore.*

*The wire crate is a most effective means to accelerate housebreaking and is the safest way to ensure that the puppy is safe when he cannot be supervised.*

**THE CRATE**

Although many dog lovers may cringe at the mere mention of the word *crate,* thinking of it as a cage or a cruel means of confinement, this handy piece of equipment can be put to good use for puppies and grown dogs alike. Even though you may love your dog to an extraordinary degree, you may not want him to have free reign of the house, particularly when you are not home to supervise him. If used properly, a crate can restrict your dog when it is not convenient to have him underfoot, *i.e.,* when guests are visiting or during your mealtimes.

A surprising number of dog owners, who originally had negative feelings about crating their dogs, have had great success using crates. The crate itself serves as a bed, provided it is furnished with bedding material, or it can be used as an indoor dog house. Not all dogs readily accept crates or being confined in them for short

*Four Paws offers a wide range of shampoos for every need: from flea and tick to medicated and many others. All shampoos are pH balanced for a gentle yet effective cleaning.*

intervals, so for these dogs, another means of restriction must be found. But for those dogs that do adjust to spending time in these structures, the crate can be useful in many ways. The animal can be confined for a few hours while you are away from home or at work, or you can bring your crated dog along with you in the car when you travel or go on vacation. Crates also prove handy as carriers whenever you have to transport a sick dog to the veterinarian.

Most crates are made of sturdy wire or plastic, and some of the collapsible models can be conveniently stored or folded so that they can be moved easily from room to room or from inside the house to the yard on a warm, sunny day. If you allow your puppy or grown dog to become acquainted with its crate by cleverly propping the door open and leaving some of his favorite toys inside, in no time he will come to regard the crate as his own doggie haven. As with a dog bed, place the crate away from drafts in a dry, warm spot; refrain from placing food and water dishes in it, as these only crowd the space and offer opportunity for spillage.

If you need to confine your puppy so that he can't get into mischief while you're not home, remember to consider the animal's needs at all times. Select a large crate, one in which the dog can stand up and move around comfortably; in fact, bigger is better in this context. Never leave the animal confined for more than a few hours at a time without letting him out to exercise, play, and, if necessary, relieve himself. Never crate a dog for ten hours, for example, unless you keep the door to the crate open so that he can get out for food and water and to stretch a bit. If long intervals of confinement are necessary, consider placing the unlatched crate in a partitioned section of your house or apartment.

Crates have become the answer for many a dog owner faced with the dilemma of either getting rid of a destructive dog or living with him despite his bad habits. People who have neither the time nor the patience to train their dogs, or to modify undesirable behavior patterns, can at least restrain their pets during the times they can't be there to supervise. So long as the crate is used in a humane fashion, whereby a dog is

*Traveling crates can provide safe and easy transport for your dog. Ventilation for travel is a most important consideration.*

confined for no more than a few hours at any one time, it can figure importantly in a dog owner's life. Show dogs, incidentally, learn at an early age that much time will be spent in and out of crates while they are on the show circuit. Many canine celebrities are kept in their crates until they are called to ringside, and they spend many hours crated to and from the shows.

## THE DOG HOUSE

These structures, often made of wood, should be sturdy and offer enough room for your dog to stretch out in when it rests or sleeps. Dog houses that are elevated or situated on a platform protect the animal from cold and dampness that may seep through the ground. For the breeds that are temperature hardy and will live outdoors, a dog house is an excellent option for daytime occupancy. Owners who cannot provide indoor accommodations for their chosen dog should consider a smaller breed since no dog should lead an exclusively outdoor existence.

If you have no option but to accommodate your dog with only an outdoor house, it will be necessary to provide him with a more elaborate house, one that really protects him from the elements. Make sure the dog's house is constructed of waterproof materials. Furnish

*The pet trade offers many commercially made dog houses and other outdoor living structures that make great temporary accommodations for your pet.*

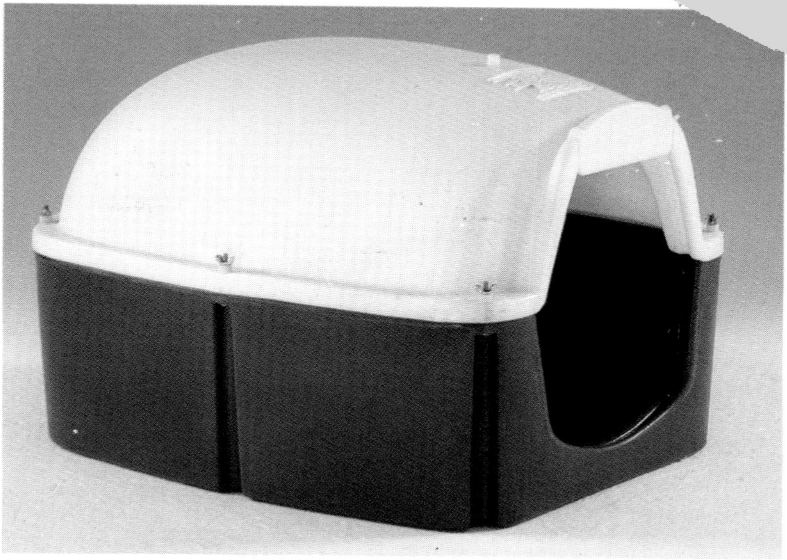

*Indoor-outdoor dog houses offer pest-free, sanitary conditions for your dog. These attractive living options can be acquired from pet shops or supply outlets.*

him with sufficient bedding to burrow into on a chilly night and provide extra insulation to keep out drafts and wet weather. Add a partition (a kind of room divider which separates the entry area from the main sleeping space) inside his house or attach a swinging door to the entrance to help keep him warm when he is inside his residence. The swinging door facilitates entry to and from the dog house, while at the same time it provides protection, particularly from wind and drafts.

Some fortunate owners whose yards are enclosed by high fencing allow their dogs complete freedom within the boundaries of their property. In these situations, a dog can leave his dog house and get all the exercise he wants. Of course such a large space requires more effort to keep it clean. An alternative to complete backyard freedom is a dog kennel or run which attaches to or surrounds the dog's house. This restricts some forms of movement, such as running, perhaps, but it does provide ample room for walking, climbing, jumping, and stretching. Another option is to fence off part of the yard and place the dog house in the enclosure. If you need to tether your dog to its house, make certain to use a fairly long lead so as not to hamper the animal's need to move and exercise his limbs.

*An anchored lead can provide efficient temporary restraint. This is not a viable substitute for a fenced-in yard and no dog should be left unsupervised on such a lead for any length of time.*

**CLEANLINESS**

No matter where your dog lives, either in or out of your home, be sure to keep him in surroundings that are as clean and sanitary as possible. His excrement should be removed and disposed of every day without fail. No dog should be forced to lie in his own feces. If your dog lives in his own house, the floor should be swept occasionally and the bedding should be changed regularly if it becomes soiled. Food and water dishes need to be scrubbed with hot water and detergent and rinsed well to remove all traces of soap. The water dish should be refilled with a supply of fresh water. The dog and his environment must be kept free of parasites (especially fleas and mosquitoes, which can carry disease) with products designed to keep these pests under control. Dog crates need frequent scrubbing, too, as do the floors of kennels and runs. Your pet must be kept clean and comfortable at all times; if you exercise strict sanitary control, you will keep disease and parasite infestation to a minimum.

**EXERCISE**

A well-balanced diet and regular medical attention from a qualified veterinarian are essential in promoting good health for your dog, but so is daily exercise to keep him fit and mentally alert. Dogs that have been confined all day while their owners are at work or school need special attention. There should be some time set aside each day for play—a romp with a family member, perhaps. Not everyone is lucky enough to let his dog run through an open meadow or along a sandy beach, but even a ten-minute walk in the fresh air will do. Dogs that are house-bound, particularly those that live in apartments, need to be walked out-of-doors after each meal so that they can relieve themselves. Owners can make this daily ritual more pleasant both for themselves and their canine companions by combining the walk with a little "roughhousing," that is to say, a bit of fun and togetherness.

Whenever possible, take a stroll to an empty lot, a playground, or a nearby park. Attach a long lead to your dog's collar, and let him run and jump and tone his body through aerobic activity. This will help him burn calories and will keep him trim, and it will also help relieve tension and stress that may have had a chance to develop while you were away all day. For people who work Monday through Friday, weekend jaunts can be especially beneficial, since there will be more time to spend with your canine friend. You might want to engage him in a simple game of fetch with a stick or a rubber ball. Even such basic tricks as rolling over, standing on the hindlegs, or jumping up (all of which can be done inside

*Four Paws Stain & Odor Remover contains active enzymes to remove tough urine stains and the odor that attracts puppies to the previously soiled area.*

the home as well) can provide additional exercise. But if you plan to challenge your dog with a real workout to raise his heart rate, remember not to push him too hard without first warming up with a brisk walk. Don't forget to "cool him down" afterwards with a rhythmic trot until his heart rate returns to normal. Some dog owners jog with their dogs or take them along on bicycle excursions.

At the very least, however, play with your dog every day to keep him in good shape physically and mentally. If you can walk him outdoors, or better yet run with him in a more vigorous activity, by all means do it. Don't neglect your pet and leave him confined for long periods without attention from you or time for exercise.

## EXERCISING FOR YOU AND YOUR DOG

Dogs are like people. They come in three weights: overweight, underweight, and the correct weight. It is fair to say that most dogs are in better shape than most humans who own them. The reason for this is that most dogs accept exercise without objection—

*The most popular in flying discs designed especially for dogs is the Nylabone Frisbee®, a toy that outlasts plastic discs by ten times. The molded dog bone on the top makes for easy retrieves by your dog.*

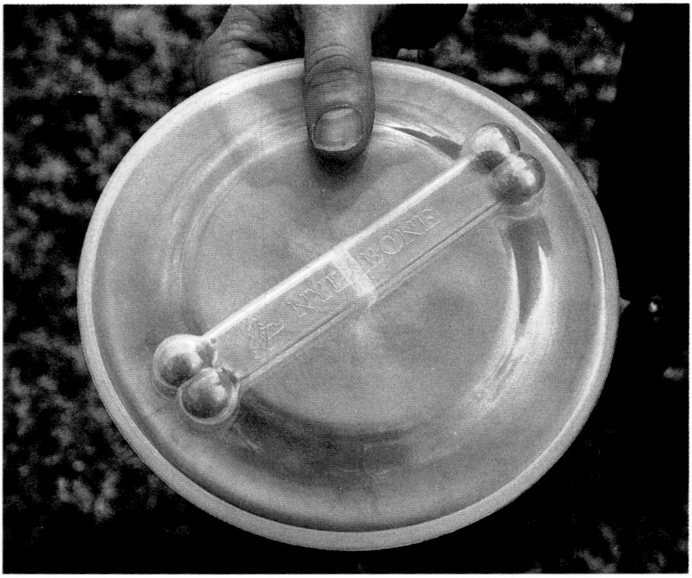

people do not! Follow your dog's lead towards exercise and the complete enjoyment of the outdoors—your dog is the ideal work-out partner. There are toys at your local pet shop which are designed just for that purpose: to allow you to play and exercise with your dog. Here are a few recommended exercise toys for you and your dog.

**Frisbee® Flying Discs®** Most dog owners capitalize on the dog's natural instinct to fetch or retrieve, and the Frisbee® flying disc is standard fare for play. The original Frisbee® is composed of polyethylene plastic, ideal for flying and great for games of catch between two humans. Since humans don't usually chew on their flying discs, there is no need for a "chew-worthy" construction material. Dogs, on the other hand, do chew on their Frisbees® and therefore should not be allowed to play with a standard original Frisbee®. These discs will be destroyed quickly by the dog and the rigid plastic can cause intestinal complications.

**Nylon Discs** More suitable for playing with dogs are the Frisbee® discs that are constructed from nylon. These durable Frisbee® discs are designed especially for dogs and the nearly indestructible manufacturing makes them ideal for aggressive chewing dogs. For play with dogs, the nylon discs called Nylabone Frisbee® are guaranteed to last ten times as long as the regular plastic Frisbee®. Owners should carefully consider the size of the nylon Frisbee® they purchase. A rule of thumb is choose the largest disc that your dog can comfortably carry. Nylabone manufactures two

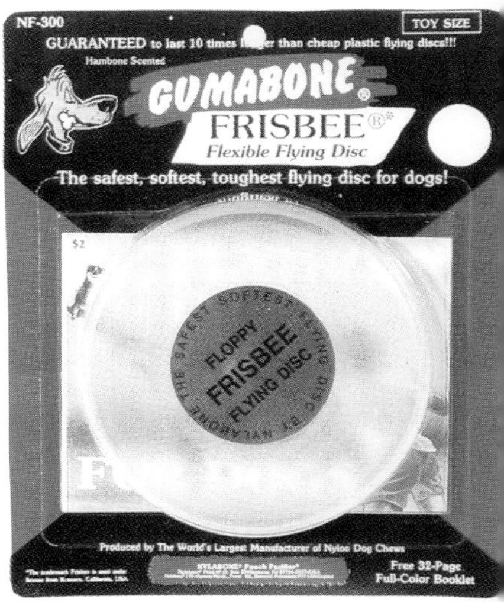


*Made of durable and flexible polyurethane, the Gumabone® Frisbees® prove chew-worthy and good-smelling to dogs. These and other Nylabone® discs are available in pet shops and other stores.*

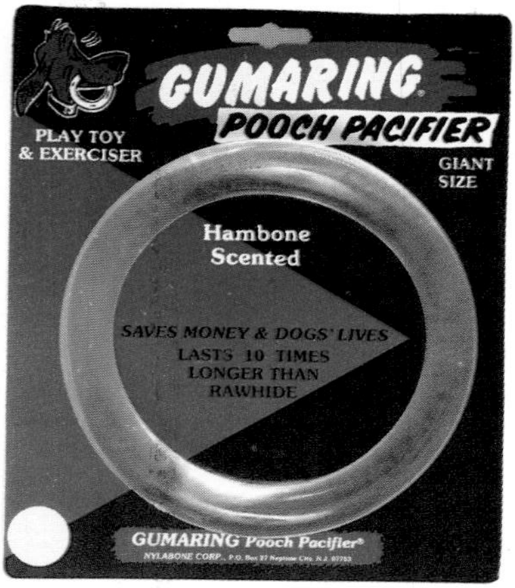


*Dogs enjoy toys they can carry around. The Gumaring® is a favorite plaything for many dogs.*

*The Tug Toy from Gumabone® is a flavorable exercise device that can be enjoyed by dog and owner.*

sizes only—toy and large—so the choice should be apparent.

**Polyurethane Flexible Floppy Flying Discs** The greatest advance in flying discs came with the manufacture of these discs from polyurethane. The polyurethane is so soft that it doesn't hurt you, your dog, or the window it might strike accidentally. The polyurethane Gumadisc® is floppy and soft. It can be folded and fits into your pocket. It is also much tougher than cheap plastics, and most pet shops guarantee that it will last ten times longer than cheap plastic discs.

Making the polyurethane discs even more suited to dog play is the fact that many of the Gumabone® Frisbee® Flexible Fly Discs have the advantage of a dog bone molded on the top. Very often a Frisbee® without the bone molded on the top is difficult for a dog to pick up when it lands on a flat surface. The molded ones enable the dog to grasp it with his mouth or turn it with his paw. Dogs love pawing at the bone and even chew on it occasionally.

This product has one further capacity—it doubles

as a temporary drinking dish while out running, hiking and playing. The Gumabone Frisbee® flyers may also be flavored or scented, besides being annealed, so your dog can find it more easily if it should get lost in woods or tall grass.

Flying discs manufactured by the Nylabone® Company may cost more than some of its imitators, but an owner can be assured that the product will last and not be quickly destroyed.

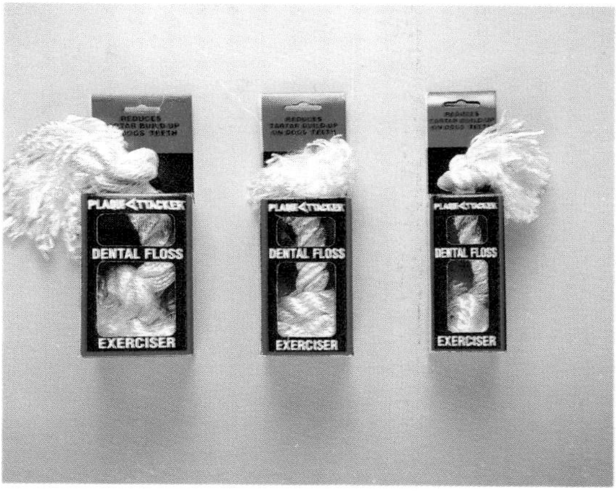


*Dental floss devices from Nylabone® serve two excellent purposes: good exercise and clean teeth.*

With most flying discs made for dogs comes an instruction booklet on how to use the disc with your canine friend. Basically, you play with the dog and the disc so the dog knows the disc belongs to him. Then you throw it continuously, increasing the distance, so that the dog fetches it and brings it back to you.

The exercise for you comes in when your dog stops fetching it, or when you have a partner. The two of you play catch. You stand as far apart as available space allows—usually 30–35 m (100 feet) is more than enough room. You throw the disc to each other, arousing your dog's interest as he tries to catch it. When the disc is dropped or veers off, the dog grabs it and brings it back (hopefully). Obviously you will have to run to catch the disc before your dog does.

There are contests held all over the world where distance, height, and other characteristics are measured competitively. Ask your local pet shop to help you locate a Frisbee® Club near you.

*Frisbee® is a trademark of the Kransco Company, California, and is used for their brand of flying disc.

**Tug Toys** A tug toy is a hard rubber, cheap plastic, or polyurethane toy which allows a dog and his owner to have a game of tug-o-war. The owner grips one end while the dog grips the other—then they pull. The polyurethane flexible tug toy is the best on the market at the present time. Your pet shop will have one to show you. The polyurethane toys are clear in color and stay soft forever. Cheap plastic tug toys are indisputably dangerous, and the hard-rubber tug toys get brittle too fast and are too stiff for most dogs; however, there *is* a difference in price—just ask the advice of any pet shop operator.

*It pays to invest in entertainment toys and exercise devices which are marketed particularly for dogs. These products outlast everyday play things and are much safer for your pet. The Gumaball® is a great example of a dog toy worth the price of admission.*

**Balls** Nobody has to tell you about playing ball with your dog. The reminder you may need is that you should not throw the ball where traffic might interfere with the dog's catching or fetching of it. The ball should not be cheap plastic (a dog's worst enemy as far as toys are concerned) but made of a substantial material. Balls made of nylon are practically indestructible, but they are very hard and must be rolled, never thrown. The same balls made of polyurethane are great—they bounce and are soft. The Nylaballs® and Gumaballs® are scented and flavored, and dogs can easily find them when lost.

Other manufacturers make balls of almost every substance, including plastic, cotton, and wood. Soft balls, baseballs, tennis balls, and so on, have all been used by dog owners who want their dogs to play with them in a game of catch. A strong caveat is that you use only those balls made especially for dogs.

## ALL DOGS NEED TO CHEW

Puppies and young dogs need something with resistance to chew on while their teeth and jaws are developing—to cut the puppy teeth, to induce growth of the permanent teeth under the puppy teeth, to assist in getting rid of the puppy teeth on time, to help the permanent teeth through the gums, to assure normal jaw development and to settle the permanent teeth solidly in the jaws.

The adult dog's desire to chew stems from the instinct for tooth cleaning, gum massage, and jaw exercise—plus the need to vent periodic doggie tensions. . . . A pacifier if you will!

Dental caries, as they affect the teeth of humans, are virtually unknown in dogs; but tartar (calculus) accumulates on the teeth of dogs, particularly at the gum line, more rapidly than on the teeth of humans. These accumulations, if not removed, bring irritation and then infection, which erode the tooth enamel and ultimately destroy the teeth at the roots. It is important that you take your dog to your local veterinarian for periodic dental examinations.

Tooth and jaw development will normally continue until the dog is more than a year old—but sometimes much longer, depending upon the dog, its chewing exercise, rate of calcium utilization and many other factors, known and unknown, which affect the development of individual dogs. Diseases, like distemper for example, may sometimes arrest development of the teeth and jaws, which may resume months or even years later.

This is why dogs, especially puppies and young dogs, will

*An artist's representation of the calculus index, ranging from index rating* **4** *(topmost drawing) through index rating* **1** *(lowest drawing).*

**4** *Buccal crown covered*
**3** *⅔ crown covered*
**2** *⅓ crown covered*
**1** *Only gingival margin covered*
**0** *No calculus evident*

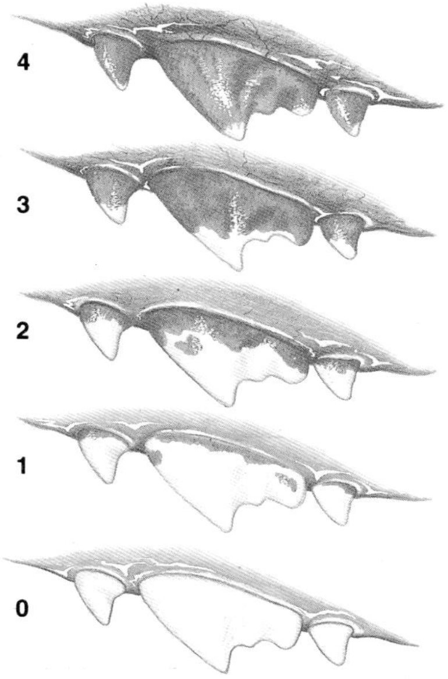

often destroy valuable property when their chewing instinct is not diverted from their owners' possessions, particularly during the widely varying critical period for young dogs. Saving your possessions from destruction, assuring proper development of teeth and jaws, providing for "interim" tooth cleaning and gum massage, and channeling doggie tensions into a non-destructive outlet are, therefore, all dependent upon the dog's having something suitable for chewing readily available when his instinct tells him to chew. If your purposes, and those of your dog, are to be accomplished, what you provide for chewing must be desirable from the doggie viewpoint, have the necessary functional qualities, and, above all, be safe.

It is very important that dogs be prohibited from chewing on anything they can break or indigestible things from which they can bite sizeable chunks. Sharp pieces, such as those from a bone which can be broken by a dog, may pierce the intestinal wall and kill. Indigestible things which can be bitten off in chunks, such as toys made of rubber compound or cheap plastic, may cause an intestinal stoppage; if not regurgitated, they are certain to bring painful death unless surgery is promptly performed.

**NATURAL CHEW BONES**

Strong natural bones, such as 4- to 8-inch lengths of round shin bone from mature beef—either the kind you can get from your butcher or one of the varieties available commercially in pet stores—may serve your dog's teething needs, if his mouth is large enough to handle them effectively, *but,* constant chewing on hard bones wears down a dog's teeth. Natural bones are very abrasive and should be used sparingly.

You may be tempted to give your puppy a smaller bone and he may not be able to break it when you do, but puppies grow rapidly and the power of their jaws constantly increases until maturity. This means that a growing dog may break one of the smaller bones at any time, swallow the pieces and die painfully before you realize what is wrong.

Many people have the mistaken notion that their dog's teeth are like those of wild carnivores or of dogs from antiquity. The teeth of wild carnivorous animals and those found in the fossils of the dog-like creatures of antiquity have far thicker and stronger enamel than those of our dogs today.

All hard natural bones are highly abrasive. If your dog is an avid chewer, natural bones may wear away his teeth

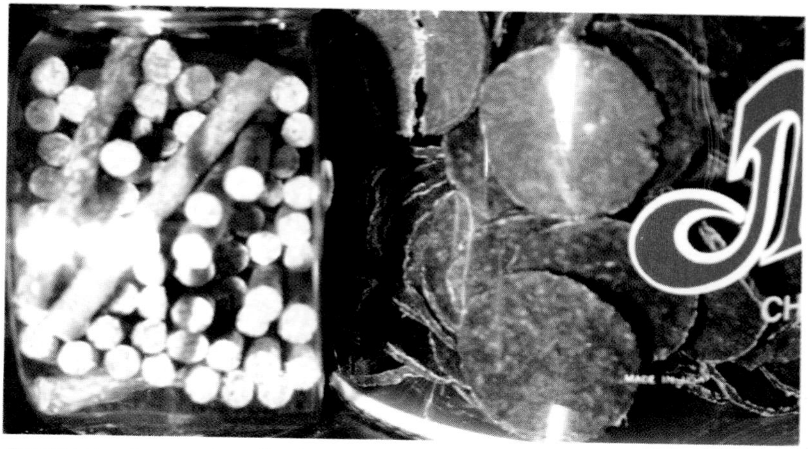


*Rawhide treats are enjoyed by dogs. Owners should be wary since rawhide can tear off in large pieces and lodge in the dog's throat or cause intestinal blockage.*

prematurely; hence, they then should be taken away from your dog when the teething purposes have been served. The badly worn, and usually painful, teeth of many mature dogs can be traced to excessive chewing on animal bones. Contrary to popular belief, knuckle bones that can be chewed up and swallowed by the dog provide little, if any, useable calcium or other nutrient. They do, however, disturb the digestion of most dogs and might cause them to vomit the nourishing food they really need.

Never give a dog your old shoe to chew on, even if you have removed all the nails or metal parts, such as lace grommets, buckles, metal arches, and so on. Rubber heels are especially dangerous, as the dog can bite off chunks, swallow them, and suffer from intestinal blockage as a result. Additionally, if the rubber should happen to have a nail imbedded in it that you cannot detect, this could pierce or tear the intestinal wall. There is always the possibility, too, that your dog may fail to differentiate between his shoe and yours and chew up a good pair while you're not looking. It is strongly recommended that you refrain from offering old shoes as chew toys, since there are much safer products available.

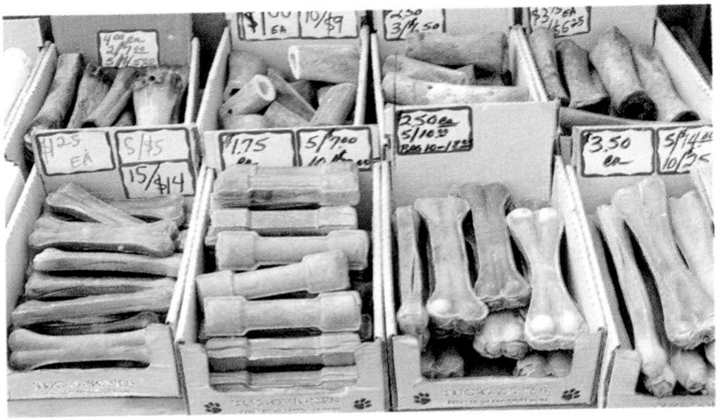

*Rawhide treats are popular choices for dogs. Owners are advised to keep an eye on their dogs whenever they are playing with rawhide.*

## RAWHIDE CHEWS

The most popular material from which dog chews are made is the hide from cows, horses, and other animals. Most of these chews are made in foreign countries where the quality of the hide is not good enough for making leather. These foreign hides may contain lead, antibiotics, arsenic, or insecticides which might be detrimental to the health of your dog...or even your children. It is not impossible that a small child will start chewing on a piece of rawhide meant for the dog! Rawhide chews do not serve the primary chewing functions very well. They are also a bit messy when wet from mouthing, and most dogs chew them up rather rapidly. They have been considered safe for dogs until recently.

Rawhide is flavorful to dogs. They like it. Currently, some veterinarians have been attributing cases of acute constipation to large pieces of incompletely digested rawhide in the intestine. Basically it is good for them to chew on, but dogs think rawhide is food. They do not play with it nor do they use it as a pacifier to relieve doggie tension. They eat it as they would any other food. This is dangerous, for the hide is very difficult for dogs to digest and swallow, and many dogs choke on large particles of rawhide that become stuck in their throats. *Before you offer your dog rawhide chews, consult your veterinarian.* Vets have a lot of experience with canine chewing devices; ask them what they recommend.

**NYLON CHEW DEVICES**

The nylon bones, especially those with natural meat and bone flavor added, are probably the most complete, safe, and economical answer to the chewing need. Dogs cannot break them nor bite off sizeable chunks; hence, they are completely safe. And being longer lasting than other things offered for the purpose, they are very economical.

Hard chewing raises little bristle-like projections on the surface of the nylon bones to provide effective interim tooth cleaning and vigorous gum massage, much in the same way your toothbrush does it for you. The little projections are raked off and swallowed in the form of thin shavings, but the chemistry of the nylon is such that they break down in the stomach fluids and pass through without effect.

The toughness of the nylon provides the strong chewing resistance needed for important jaw exercise and effective help for the teething functions; however, there is no tooth wear because nylon is non-abrasive. Being inert, nylon does not

*Annealed nylon and polyurethane chew toys are recommended by veterinarians as proven-safe and effective canine chew devices.*

*Polyurethane bones come in many colors and sizes. The Rainbows collection from Gumabone® adds flair to any dog's dental hygiene program.*

support the growth of microorganisms, and it can be washed in soap and water or sterilized by boiling or in an autoclave.

There are a great variety of Nylabone® products available that veterinarians recommend as safe and healthy for your dog or puppy to chew on. These Nylabone® Pooch Pacifiers® usually don't splinter, chip, or break off in large chunks; instead, they are frizzled by the dog's chewing action, and this creates a toothbrush-like surface that cleanses the teeth and massages the gums. At the same time, these hard-nylon therapeutic devices channel doggie tension and chewing frustation into constructive rather than destructive behavior. The original nylon bone (Nylabone®) is not a toy and dogs use it only when in need of pacification. Keeping a bone in each of your dog's recreation rooms is the best method of providing the requisite pacification. Unfortunately, many nylon chew products have been copied. These inferior quality copies are sold in supermarkets and other chain stores. The really good products are sold only through veterinarians, pet shops, grooming salons and places where the sales people really know something about dogs. The good products have the flavor impregnated *into* the bone. This makes the taste last longer. The smell is undetectable to humans. The artificial bones which have a strong odor are poor-quality bones with the odor sprayed on to impress the dog owner (not the dog)! These heavily scented dog toys may impart the odor to your carpets or furniture if an odor-sprayed bone lies there wet from a dog's chewing on it.

## FLOSS OR LOSS!

Most dentists relay that brushing daily is just not enough. In order to prevent unnecessary tooth loss, flossing is essential. For dogs, human dental floss is not the answer—however, canine dental devices are available. The Nylafloss® is a revolutionary product that is designed to save dogs teeth and keep them healthy. Even though your dogs won't believe you, Nylafloss® is not a toy but rather a most effective agent in removing destructive plaque between the teeth and *beneath* the gum line where gum disease begins. Gentle tugging is all that is necessary to activate the Nylafloss®. These 100% inert nylon products are guaranteed to outlast rawhide chews by ten times and are available for sale at all pet shops.

## THE IMPORTANCE OF PREVENTION

In order to get to the root of canine dentistry problems, it is important for owners to realize that no less than 75% of all canine dental health problems, serious enough to require a vet's assistance, and nearly 98% of all canine teeth lost are attributable to periodontal disease. Periodontal disease not only mars the teeth but also the gums and other buccal tissue in the mouth. Severe cases of periodontal disease involve resultant bacterial toxins which are absorbed into the blood

*The Nylafloss® cannot cure tooth decay, but it is an optimum decay-prevention device. Make your dog's playtime a healthy time and invest in your pet's future.*

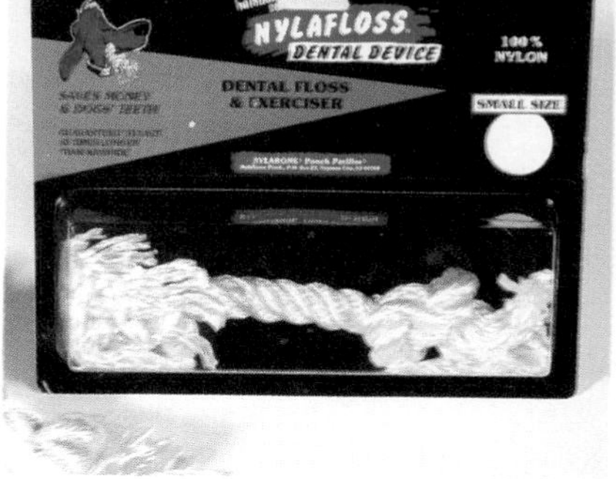

stream and cause permanent damage to the heart and kidneys. In the infected mouth, teeth are loosened; tartar, unsightly and bad smelling, accumulates heavily; and the dog experiences a complete loss of appetite. Long-standing periodontitis can also manifest itself in simple symptoms such as diarrhea and vomiting.

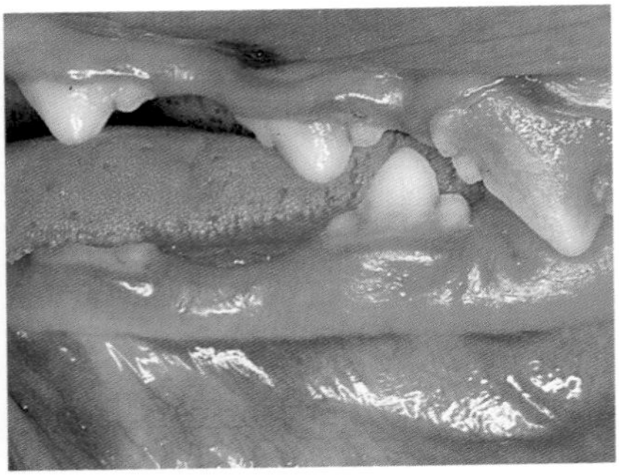

*The moderate calculus build-up on this dog's teeth reflects a certain neglect by the owner. Providing a safe chew item like the Gumabone® can help save your dog's teeth.*

Periodontal disease deserves the attention of every dog owner—a dog's teeth are extremely important to his ongoing health. The accumulation of plaque, food matter mixed with saliva attaching itself to the tooth surface, is a sure sign of potential bacteria build-up. As toxic material gathers, the bone surrounding the teeth erodes. If plaque and calculus continue to reside without attention, bacteria-fighting cells will form residual pus at the root of the teeth, dividing the gum from the tooth. The debris is toxic and actually kills the buccal tissue. This is a most undesirable situation, as hardened dental calculus is one of the most direct causative agents of periodontitis.

In actuality, the disease is a result of a number of contributing factors. Old age, a diet comprised solely of soft or semi-soft foods, dental tartar, constant chewing of hair and even coprophagy (the eating of stool) are among the most common contributors.

Just as regular dental visits and brushing are necessary for humans, regular hygienic care and veterinary check-ups can help control tooth problems in canines. Involved and expensive routines can be performed on the affected, neglected mouth and teeth if decay has begun eroding the enamel and infecting the gums. Cleaning, polishing, and scaling are routine to remove calculus build-up.

Owners must claim responsibility for their dog's health, and tooth care is no small aspect of the care required. Daily brushing with a salt/baking soda solution is the best answer, but many owners find this tedious or just too difficult to perform. The simpler and more proven effective way to avoid, reduce, and fight periodontal disease and calculus build-up is giving the dog regular access to a thermoplastic polymer chew device. The Gumabone® products are the only scientifically proven line that offers the desired protection from calculus and tartar build-up.

## CANINE DENTAL BREAKTHROUGH

The independent research of Dr. Andrew Duke, D.V.M., reveals that 70% of the dogs that regularly use Gumabone® experience a reduction of calculus build-up. This find is a breakthrough for the dog world, since the Gumabone® has already resided in the toy boxes of many dogs as their favorite play item. Little did owners know previously that their dogs were gaining entertainment and unparalleled dental treatment at the same time. Dr. Duke writes: "There is little debate left that dental calculus is an excellent indicator of periodontal health in the dog, just as it is in humans. "Calculus does not cause gingivitis and periodontitis, but the plaque and bacteria that cause periodontitis are responsible for the mineral precipitation we know as 'calculus.' All veterinarians who have made a study of dogs' oral health have noticed the middle aged dog who actively chews with excellent gingival health. Many of these dogs that chew

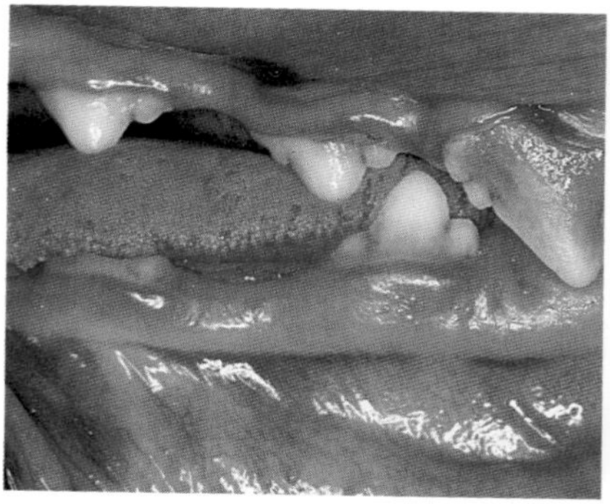

*Regular use of the Gumabone® chew products can significantly reduce plaque build-up.*

*Teeth of an infected dog showing little to no plaque accumulation after professional cleaning.*

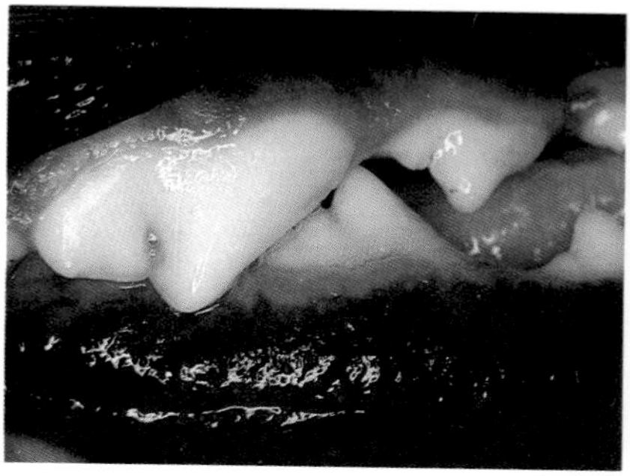

hard substances regularly wear the cusps down and even may expose the pulp cavity faster than secondary dentin can be formed. Often these "excellent chewers" are presented with slab fractures of the premolars or apical abcesses.

"The challenge then becomes to find a substance which is effective in removing calculus and plaque but does not wear the enamel excessively. In an attempt to duplicate the chewstuffs enjoyed by dogs in the wild, researchers have used bovine tracheas to demonstrate the inhibition of plaque and gingivitis. Very little else has been done in veterinary medicine to establish a scientific basis for evaluating chewstuffs.

"In the human field it is generally accepted (incorrectly) that fibrous foodstuffs and diet have no effect on oral health. This is a moot point since the practice of brushing is by far a more efficient technique of preventing plaque accumulation, calculus and periodontal disease. Studies in human subjects failed to find any benefits in eating apples, raw carrots, etc. If people are not allowed to brush, it is difficult to

*The clean healthy teeth that are desired in dogs should inspire owners to work towards better dental hygiene.*

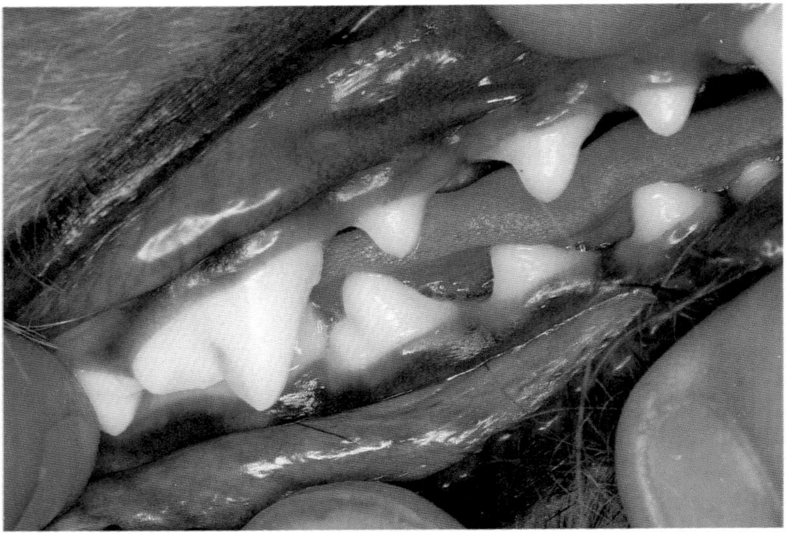

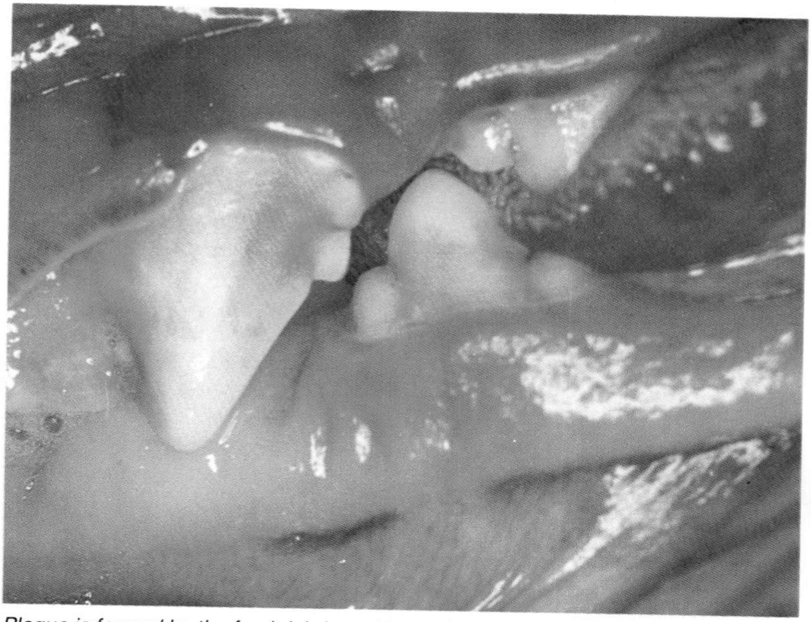

*Plaque is formed by the food debris and bacterial deposits left on teeth. Due to the high carbon dioxide and pH levels in the mouth, minerals precipitate quickly on the plaque to form calculus.*

conduct clinical trials of more than one week.

"The increased awareness of animals' dental health of recent years has resulted in most veterinary practitioners' recommending some kind of chewstuff to their dog owners. To meet this market demand, there has been a stampede into the market by vendors ready to promote their products. The veterinarian is furnished no scientific data, but is asked to promote rawhide, bounce, and squeaky toys. How would our human colleagues handle this situation? Can Listerine® say that it prevents colds, but not support the claim? Can "Tartar Control Crest®" or "Colgate Tartar Control Formula®" be sold if it is not proven that it does in fact reduce tartar? Of course not.

"To this end, the following study was made.

"*Method:* Twenty dogs of different breeds and age were selected from a veterinary

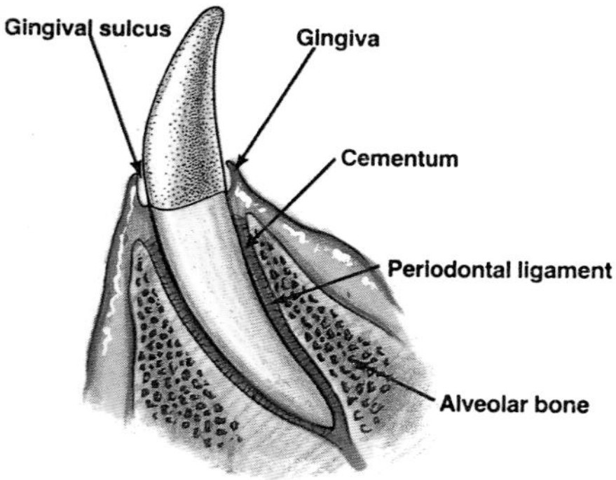


*Comparative look at healthy gums* (above) *and affected gums* (below) *in a dog's mouth. Instinctively dogs need to massage their gums—and the Gumabone® can satisfy this doggie craving.*

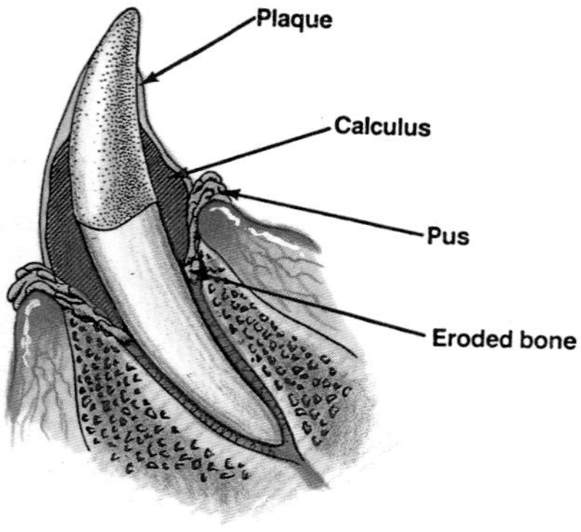


practice's clientele. Although most were from multiple pet households, none were colony dogs. The owners were asked if they would allow their dogs to be anesthetized for two prophylactic cleanings which included root planing, polishing, and gingival debridement necessary to insure good oral hygiene.

"The dogs were divided into two groups of 10. Their teeth were cleaned and their calculus index converted to 0. One group was allowed only their normal dry commercial dog ration for 30 days. The other was allowed to have free choice access to Gumabone® products of the appropriate size.

"After 30 days, photoslides were made of the upper 3rd premolar, upper 4th premolar, and the lower 4th premolar on both sides of the dog's mouth. The dogs were again subjected to a prophylactic cleaning and the group reversed. After the second 30 days, photoslides were again made. A total of six teeth in each mouth were evaluated on each dog. This was 80 slides representing 240 teeth."

Fourteen out of 20 dogs (or 70%) experienced a reduction in calculus build-up by regularly using the Gumabone® product. These products are available in a variety of sizes (for different

*Nylabone® and Gumabone® offer a new option for the choosy canine–chicken-flavored bones. Entertainment and pearly white teeth have never been better acquainted.*

size dogs) and designed in interesting shapes: bones, balls, knots and rings (and even a tug toy). The entertainment value of the Gumabone® products is but an added advantage to the fighting of tooth decay and periodontitis. The products are ham-flavored and made of a thermoplastic polymer that is designed to outlast by ten times any rawhide, rubber or vinyl chew product, none of which can promise the proven benefit of the Gumabone®.

If your dog is able to chew apart a Gumabone®, it is probable that you provided him with a bone that is too small for him. Replace it with a larger one and the problem should not rematerialize. Economically, the Gumabone® is a smart choice, even without comparing it to the cost of extensive dental care.

Of course, nothing can *substitute* for periodic

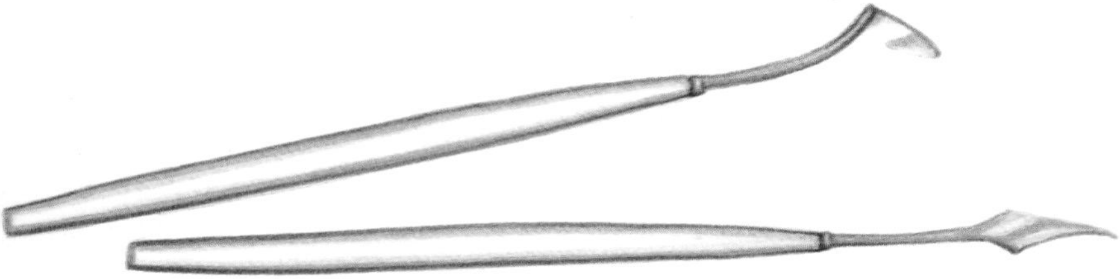

*In cases of bad neglect, scaling a dog's teeth can help to save or salvage affected teeth. Your veterinarian can perform this procedure.*

professional attention to your dog's teeth and gums, no more than your toothbrush can replace your dentist. Have your dog's teeth cleaned by your veterinarian at least once a year—twice a year is better—and he will be healthier, happier, and a far more pleasant companion.

Gumabones® are available through veterinarians and pet shops.

*Canine tooth brushes are designed to allow access to the most hard-to-reach places in the canine mouth. Accustom your dog to brushing from puppyhood.*

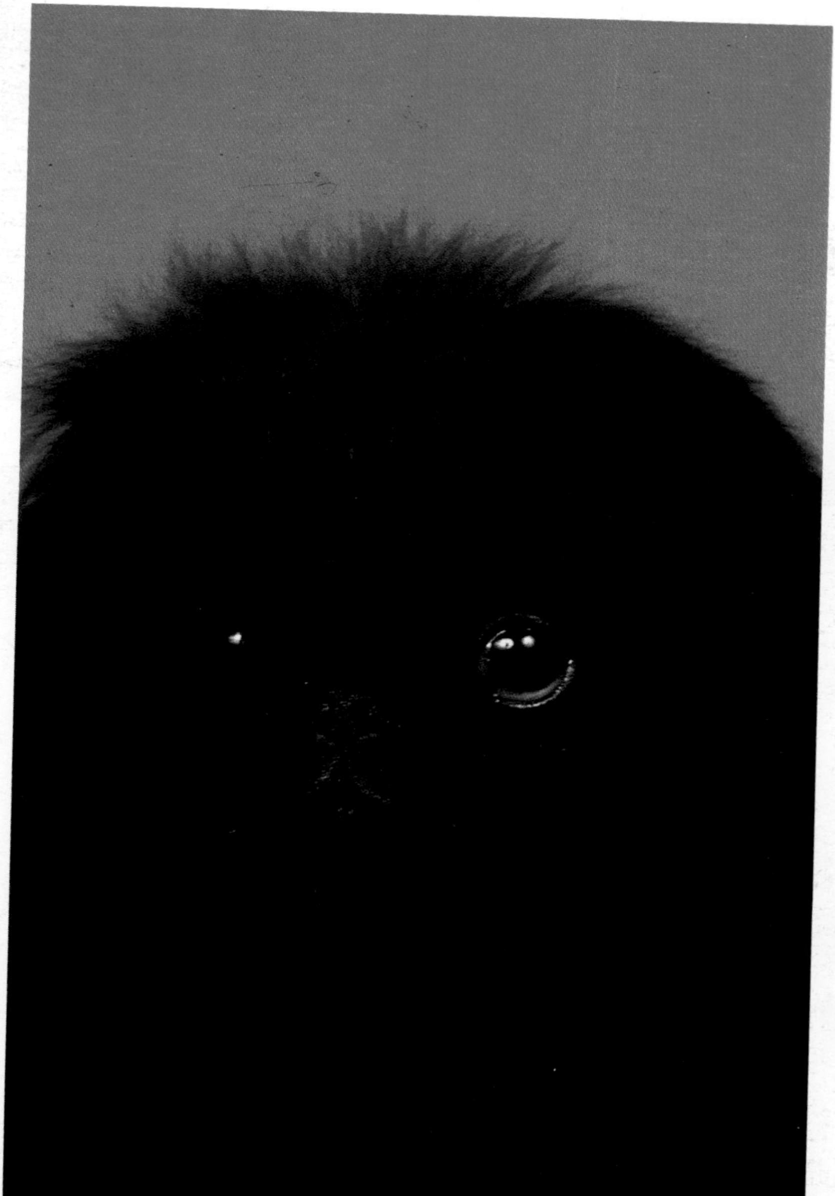

*Your Pekingese is the aristocrat of dogdom. Be sure to care for him as such, and he will provide you with many wonderful years of loving companionship.*

## HOUSEBREAKING

The new addition to your family may already have received some basic house training before his arrival in your home. If he has not, remember that a puppy will want to relieve himself about half a dozen times a day; it is up to you to specify where and when he should "do his business." Housebreaking is your first training concern and should begin the moment you bring the puppy home.

Ideally, puppies should be taken outdoors after meals, as a full stomach will exert pressure on the bladder and colon. What goes into the dog must eventually come out; the period

*Four Paws Wee-Wee Pads are scientifically treated to attract puppies when nature calls. The plastic lining prevents damage to floors and carpets.*

after his meal is the most natural and appropriate time. When he eliminates, he should be praised, for this will increase the likelihood of the same thing happening after every meal. He should also be encouraged to use the same area and will probably be attracted to it after frequent use.

Some veterinarians maintain that a puppy can learn to urinate and defecate on command, if properly trained. The advantage of this conditioning technique is that your pet will associate the act of elimination with a particular word of your choice rather than with a particular time or place which might not always be convenient or available. So whether you are visiting an unfamiliar place or don't want to go outside with your dog in sub-zero temperatures, he will still be able to relieve himself when he hears the specific command word. Elimination will occur after this "trigger" phrase or word sets up a conditioned reflex in the dog, who will eliminate anything contained in his bladder or bowel upon hearing it. The shorter the word, the more you can repeat it and imprint it on your dog's memory.

Your chosen command word should be given simultaneously with the sphincter opening events in order to achieve perfect and rapid conditioning. This is why it is important to familiarize yourself with the tell-tale signs preceding your puppy's elimination process. Then you will be prepared to say the word at the crucial moment. There is usually a sense of

*Crates assist in house-training the puppy. The dog's natural instinct is never to soil his sleeping area.*

urgency on the dog's part; he may follow a sniffing and circling pattern which you will soon recognize. It is important to use the command in his usual area only when you know the puppy can eliminate, i.e., when his stomach or bladder is full. He will soon learn to associate the act with the word. One word of advice, however, if you plan to try out this method: never use the puppy's name or any other word which he might frequently hear about the house—you can imagine the result!

Finally, remember that any training takes time. Such a conditioned response can be obtained with intensive practice with any normal, healthy dog over six weeks of age. Even Pavlov's salivating dogs required fifty repetitions before the desired response was achieved. Patience and persistence will eventually produce results—do not lose heart!

Indoors, sheets of newspapers can be used to cover the specific area where your dog should relieve himself. These should be placed some distance away from his sleeping and feeding area, as a puppy

*Begin the training of your Pekingese pups right away. Patience and persistence will produce a well-behaved pet.*

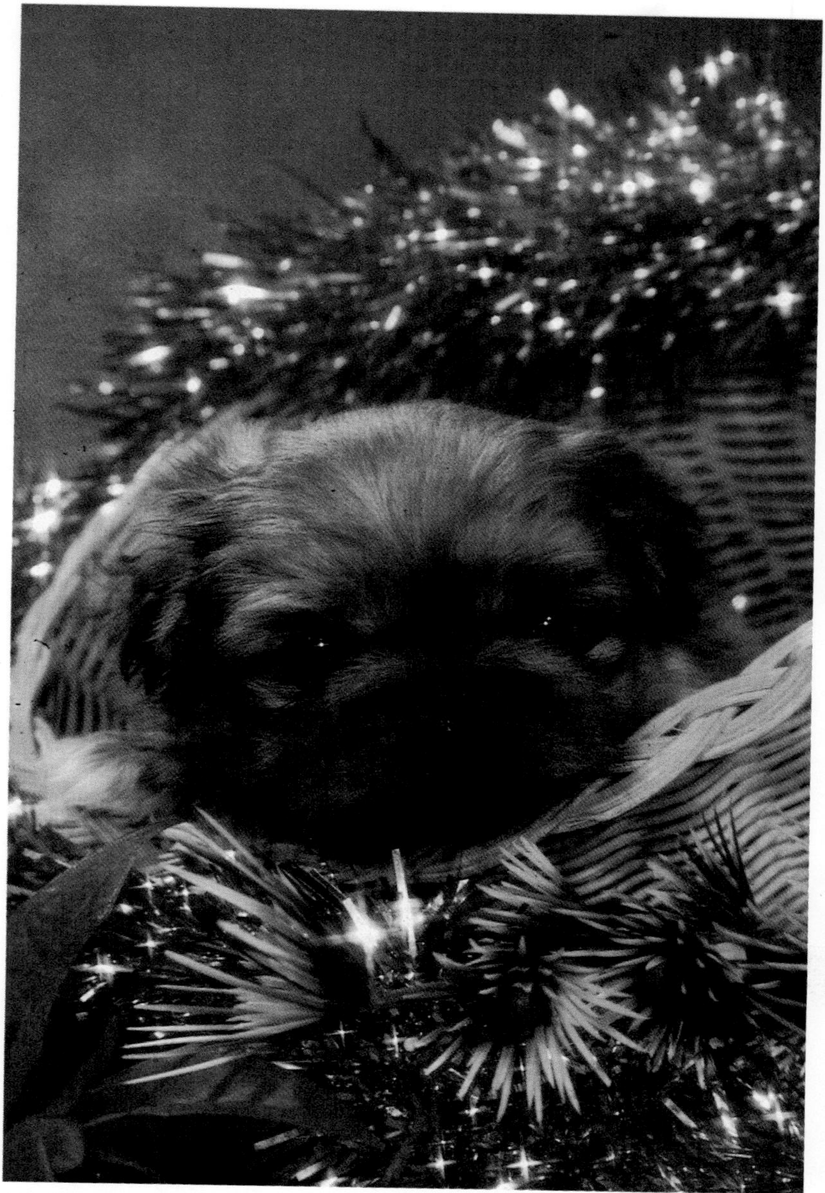

*Holidays are not the best time to bring your Pekingese pup home. The excitement and visitors may be too much for a puppy to handle. Plan to make your Peke's arrival as relaxed and routine as possible.*

*The choke collar and walking lead are commonly used in training.*

will not urinate or defecate where he eats. When the newspapers are changed, the bottom papers should be placed on top of the new ones in order to reinforce the purpose of the papers by scent as well as by sight. The puppy should be praised during or immediately after he has made use of this particular part of the room. Each positive reinforcement increases the possibility of his using that area again.

When he arrives, it is advisable to limit the puppy to one room, usually the kitchen, as it most likely has a linoleum or easily washable floor surface. Given the run of the house, the sheer size of the place will seem overwhelming and confusing and he might leave his "signature" on your furniture or clothes! There will be time later to familiarize him gradually with his new surroundings.

## PATIENCE, PERSISTENCE, AND PRAISE

As with a human baby, you must be patient, tolerant, and understanding of your pet's mistakes, making him feel loved and wanted, not rejected and isolated. You wouldn't hit a baby for soiling his diapers, as you would realize that he was not yet able to control his bowel movements; be as compassionate with your canine infant. Never rub his nose in his excreta. Never indulge in the common practice of punishing him with a rolled-up newspaper. Never hit a puppy with your hand. He will only become "hand-shy" and learn to fear you. Usually the punishment is meted out sometime after the offense and loses its efficacy, as the bewildered dog cannot connect the two events. Moreover, by association, he will soon learn to be afraid of you and anything to do with newspapers—including, perhaps, that area where he is *supposed* to relieve himself!

Most puppies are eager to please. Praise, encouragement, and reward (particularly the food variety) will produce far better results than any scolding or physical punishment. Moreover, it is far better to dissuade your puppy from doing certain things, such as chewing on chair legs or other furniture, by making those objects particularly distasteful to him. Some pet shops stock bitter apple sprays or citronella compounds for application to furniture legs. These products are generally safer than old-fashioned home remedies. An owner may soon discover that application of these products may indeed make it seem as if

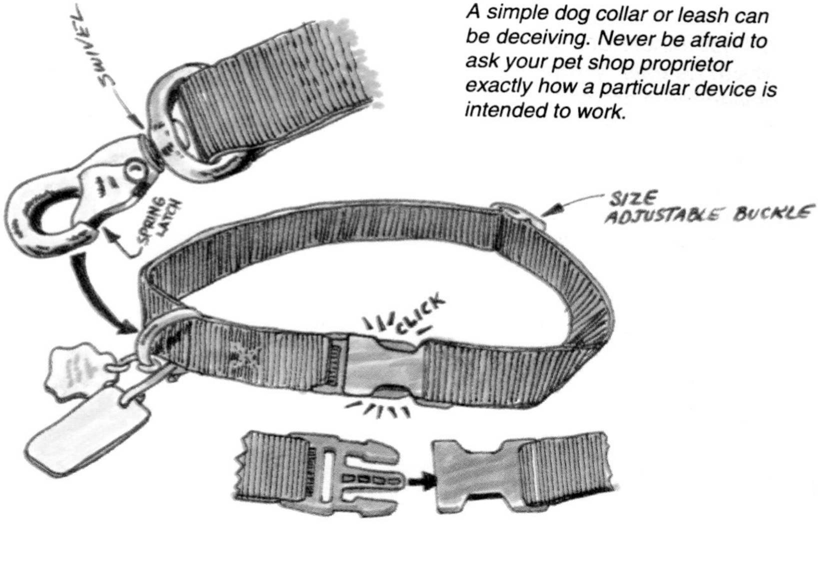


*A simple dog collar or leash can be deceiving. Never be afraid to ask your pet shop proprietor exactly how a particular device is intended to work.*

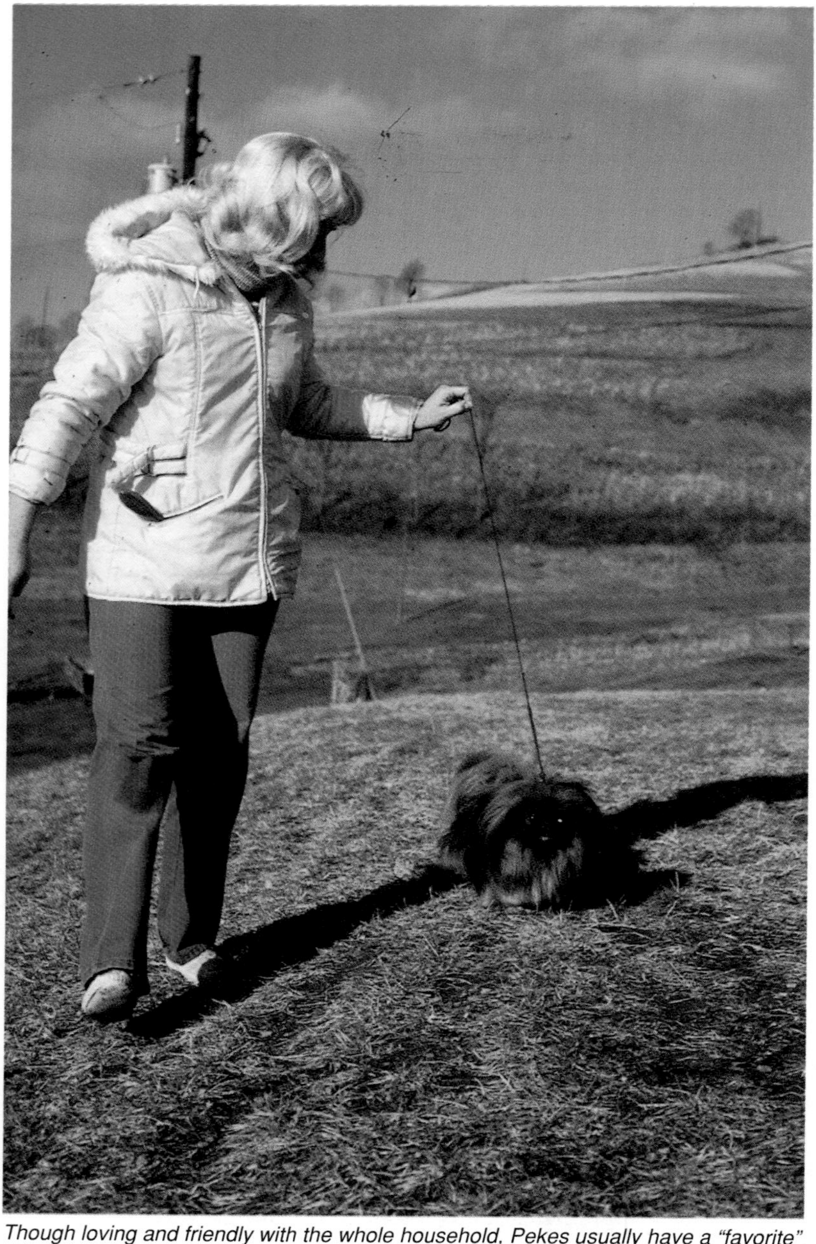

*Though loving and friendly with the whole household, Pekes usually have a "favorite" family member whom they will obey more readily.*

the object itself was administering the punishment whenever he attempted to chew it. He probably wouldn't need a second reminder and your furniture will remain undamaged.

Remember that the reason a dog has housebreaking or behavior problems is because his owner has allowed them to develop. This is why you must begin as you intend to continue, letting your dog know what is acceptable and unacceptable behavior. It is also important that you be consistent in your demands; you cannot feed him from the dining room table one day and then punish him when he begs for food from your dinner guests.

## TRAINING

You will want the newest member of your family to be welcomed by everyone; this will not happen if he urinates in every room of the house or barks all night! He needs training in the correct forms of behavior in this new human world. You cannot expect your puppy to become the perfect pet overnight. He needs your help in

*The tiny Pekingese has very clean habits, and is easily housebroken.*

his socialization process. Training greatly facilitates and enhances the relationship of the dog to his owner and to the rest of society. A successfully trained dog can be taken anywhere and behave well with anyone. Indeed, it is that one crucial word—*training*—which can transform an aggressive animal into a peaceful, well-behaved pet. Now, how does this "transformation" take place?

## WHEN AND HOW TO TRAIN

Like housebreaking, training should begin as soon as the puppy enters the house. The formal training sessions should be short but frequent, for example, ten to fifteen minute periods three times a day. These are much more effective than long, tiring sessions of half an hour which might soon become boring. You are building your relationship with your puppy during these times, so make them as enjoyable as possible. It is a good idea to have these sessions *before* the puppy's meal, not after it when he wouldn't feel like exerting himself; the dog will then associate something pleasurable with his training sessions and look forward to them.

*A choke collar can be an effective training tool when properly used.*

## THE COLLAR AND LEASH

Your puppy should become used to a collar and leash as soon as possible. If he is very young, a thin, choke-chain collar can be used, but you will need a larger and heavier one for training when he is a little older. Remember to have his name and address on an identification tag attached to his collar, as you don't want to lose your pet if he should happen to leave your premises and explore the neighborhood!

Let the puppy wear his collar until he is used to how it feels. After a short time he will soon become accustomed to it and you can attach the leash. He might resist your attempts to lead him or simply sit down and refuse to budge. Fight him for a few minutes, tugging on the leash if necessary, then let him relax for the day. He won't be trained until he learns that he must obey the pull under any circumstance, but this will take a few sessions. Remember that a dog's period of concentration is short, so *little* and *often* is the wisest course of action—and patience is the password to success.

## GIVING COMMANDS

When you begin giving your puppy simple commands, make them as short as possible and use the same word with the same meaning at all times, for example, "Heel," "Sit," and "Stay." You must be consistent; otherwise your puppy will become confused. The dog's name should prefix all commands to attract his attention. Do not become impatient with him however many times you have to repeat your command.

A good way to introduce the "Come" command is by calling the puppy when his meal is ready. Once this is learned, you can call your pet to you at will, always remembering to praise him for his prompt obedience. This "reward," or positive

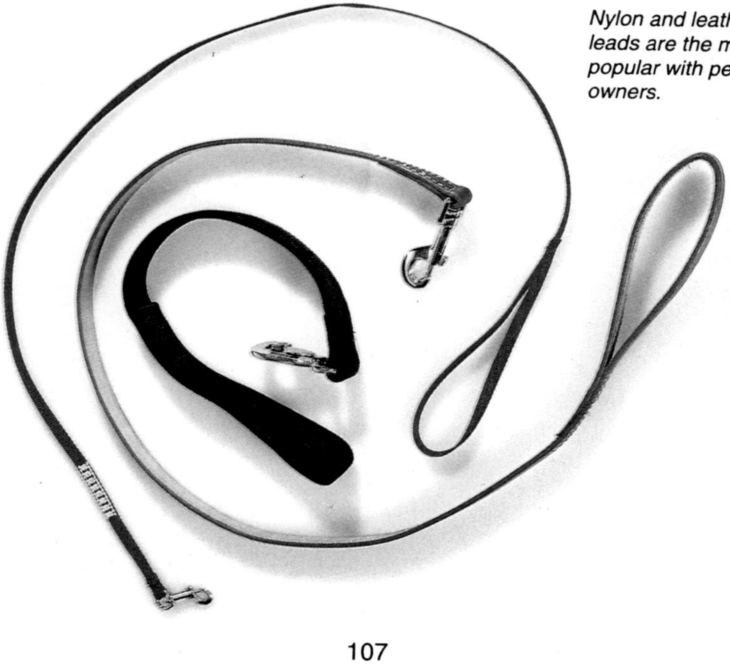

*Nylon and leather leads are the most popular with pet owners.*

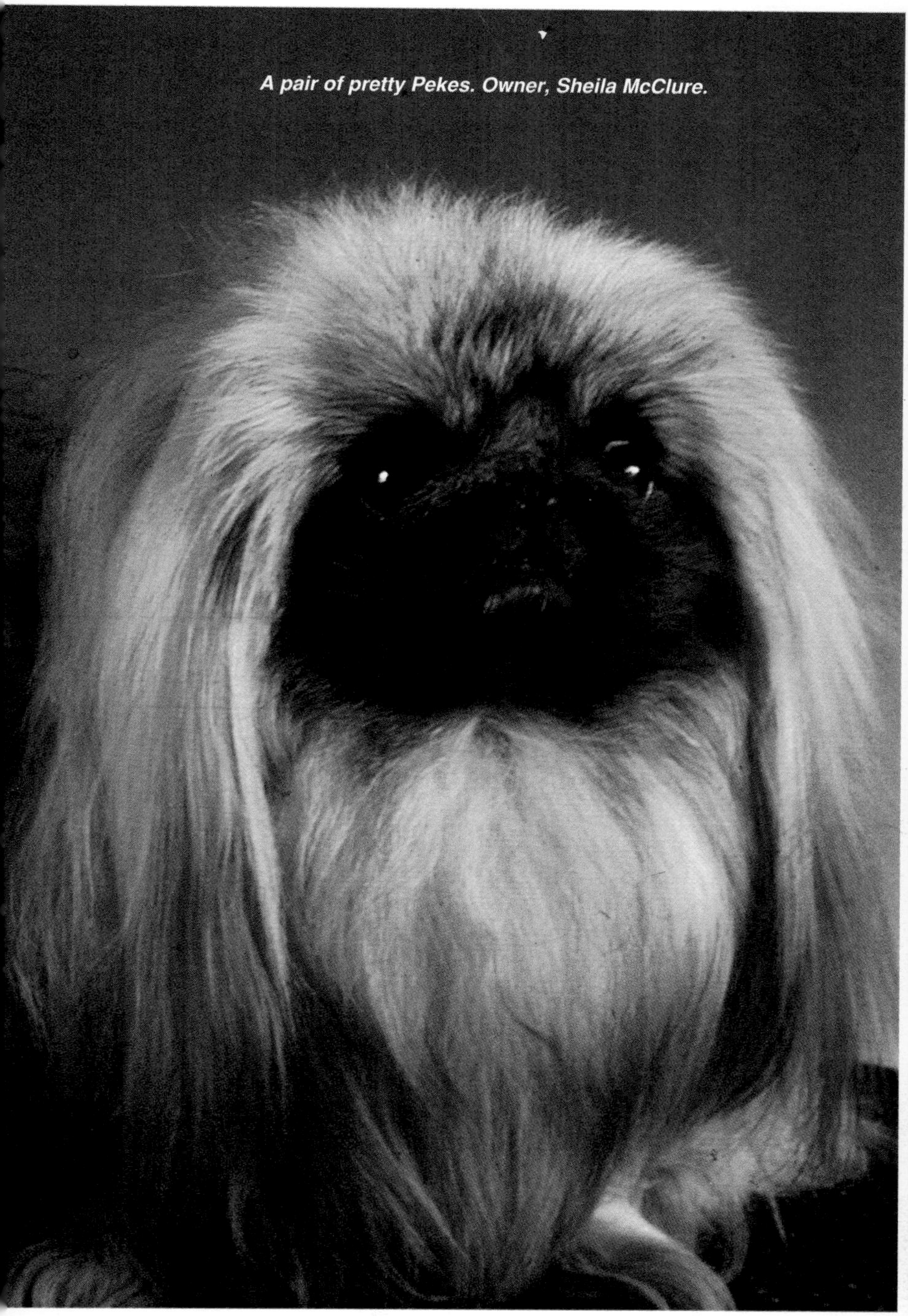

*A pair of pretty Pekes. Owner, Sheila McClure.*

reinforcement, is such a crucial part of training that a Director of the New York Academy of Dog Training constructed his whole teaching program upon the methods of "Love, Praise, and Reward." Incidentally, if you use the command "Come," use it every time. Don't switch to "Come here" or "Come boy," as this will only confuse your dog.

*Guaranteed by the manufacturer to stop any dog, any size, any weight from ever pulling again. It's like having power steering for your dog.*

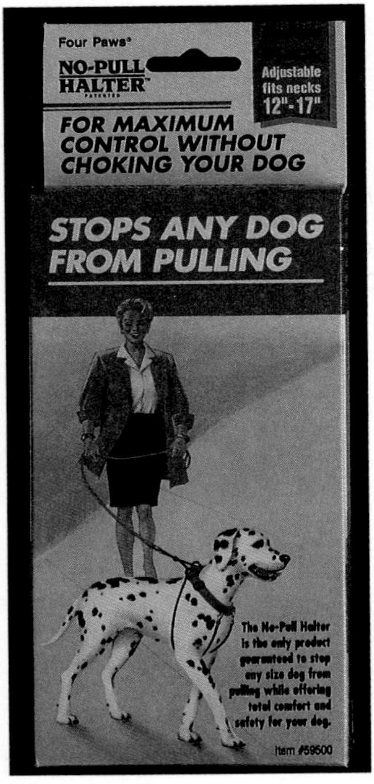


It is worth underlining the fact that punishment is an ineffective teaching technique. We have already seen this in housebreaking. For example, if your pup should run away, it would be senseless to beat him when he eventually returns; he would only connect the punishment with his return, not with running away! In addition, it is unwise to call him to you to punish him, as he will soon learn not to respond when you call his name.

## SOME SPECIFIC COMMANDS

**"Sit"** This is one of the easiest and most useful commands for your dog to learn, so it is a good idea to begin with it. The only equipment required is a leash, a collar, and a few tasty tidbits. Take your dog out for some exercise before his meal. After about five minutes, call him to you, praise him when he arrives, and slip his collar on him. Hold the leash tightly in your right hand; this should force the dog's head up and focus his attention on you. As you say "Sit" in a loud, clear voice, with your left hand press steadily on his rump until he is in a sitting position. As soon as he is in the correct position, praise him and give him the tidbit you have in your hand. Now wait a few minutes to let him rest and repeat the routine. Through repetition, the dog soon associates the word with the act. Never make the lesson too long. Eventually your praise will be reward enough for your puppy. Other methods to teach this command exist, but this one, executed with care and moderation, has proven the most effective.

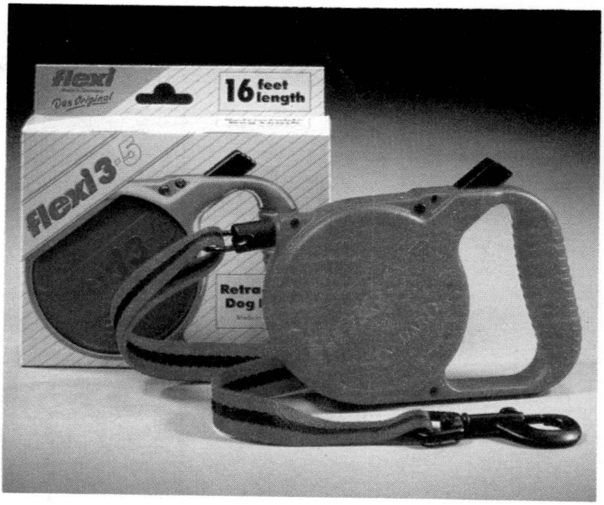


*Great for the athletic dog and less-active owner are commercially designed retractable leads which give the dog much more freedom when exercising in an open field or cleared area. Photo courtesy of Flexi USA, Inc.*

**"Sit-Stay/ Stay"** To teach your pet to remain in one place or "stay" on your command, first of all order him to the sitting position at your side. Lower your left hand with the flat of your palm in front of his nose and your fingers pointing downwards. Hold the leash high and taut behind his head so that he cannot move. Speak the command "Sit-stay" and, as you are giving it, step in front of him. Repeat the command and tighten the leash so the animal cannot follow you. Walk completely around him, repeating the command and keeping him motionless by holding the leash at arm's length above him to check his movement. When he remains in this position for about fifteen seconds, you can begin the second part of the training. You will have to exchange the leash for a nylon cord or rope about twenty to thirty feet long. Repeat the whole routine from the beginning and be ready to prevent any movement towards you with a sharp "Sit-stay." Move around him in ever-widening circles until you are about fifteen feet away from him. If he still remains seated, you can pat yourself on the back! One useful thing to remember is that the dog makes associations with what you say, how you say it, and what you do while you are saying it. Give this command in a firm, clear tone of voice, perhaps using an admonishing forefinger raised, warning the dog to "stay."

**"Heel"** When you walk your dog, you should hold the leash firmly in your right hand. The dog should walk on your left so you have the leash crossing your body. This enables you to have greater control over the dog.

Let your dog lead you for the first few moments so that he fully understands that freedom can be his if he goes about it properly. He already knows that when he wants to go outdoors the leash and collar are necessary, so he has respect for the leash. Now, if he starts to pull in one direction while walking, all you do is *stop walking.* He will walk a few steps and then find that he can't walk any further. He will then turn and look into your face. *This is the crucial point!* Just stand there for a moment and stare right back at him . . . now walk another ten feet and stop again. Again your dog will probably walk to the end of the leash, find he can't go any further, and turn around and look again. If he starts to pull and jerk, just stand there. After he quiets

*Grooming is part of the training process. Begin brushing your Peke as a pup and he will easily become accustomed to a regular grooming schedule.*

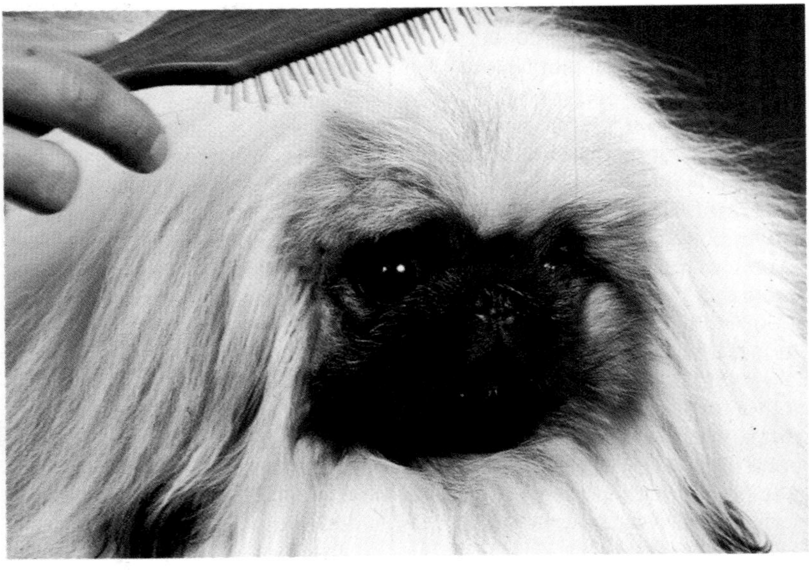

*Make sure your Pekingese has a proper-fitting collar and always use a leash when training outdoors.*

down, bend down and comfort him, as he may be frightened. Keep up this training until he learns not to outwalk you.

Once the puppy obeys the pull of the leash, half of your training is accomplished. "Heeling" is a necessity for a well-behaved dog, so teach him to walk beside you, head even with your knee. Nothing looks sadder than a big dog taking his helpless owner for a walk. It is annoying to passers-by and other dog owners to have a large dog, however friendly, bear down on them and entangle dogs, people, and packages.

To teach your dog, start off walking briskly, saying "Heel" in a firm voice. Pull back with a sharp jerk if he lunges ahead, and if he lags repeat the command and tug on the leash, not allowing him to drag behind. After the dog has learned to heel at various speeds on leash, you can remove it and practice heeling free, but have it ready to snap on again as soon as he wanders.

**"Come"** Your dog has already learned to come to you when you call his name. Why? Because you only call him when his food is ready or when you wish to play with him or praise him. Outdoors such a response is more difficult to achieve, if he is happily playing by himself or with other dogs, so he must be trained to come to you when he is called. To teach him to come, let him reach the end of a long lead, then give the command, gently pulling him towards you at the same time. As soon as he associates the word *come* with the action of moving towards you, pull only when he does not respond immediately. As he starts to come, move back to make him learn that he must come from a distance as well as when he is close to you. Soon you may be able to practice without a leash, but if he is slow to come or actively disobedient, go to him and pull him toward you, repeating the command. Always remember to reward his successful completion of a task.

**"Down"** Teaching the "down" command ideally begins while your dog is still a pup. During puppyhood your dog frequently will lie down, as this position is one of the dog's most natural positions. Invest some time, and keep close watch over your pup. Each time he begins to lie, repeat in a low convincing tone the word "down." If for the first day of training, you concur a majority of the dog's sitting with your commands and continue with reinforcement and moderate praise your pup should conquer the "down" command in no time.

Teaching the "down" command to a mature dog likely will require more effort. Although the lying position is still natural to a dog, his being forced into it is not. Some dogs may react with fear, anger, or confusion. Others may accept the process and prove quick learners. Have your dog sit and face you. If he is responsive and congenial, gently take his paws, and slowly pull them towards you; give the "down" command as he approaches the proper position. Repeat several times: moderate reinforcement of this procedure should prove rewardingly successful.

For the dog that responds with anger or aggression, attach a lead (and a muzzle) and have the dog sit facing you at a close distance. There should be a J-loop formed by the lead. With moderate force, relative to the size and strength of your dog, step on the J-loop, forcing the dog down, while repeating the command "down" in a low forceful tone. When the dog is down, moderate praise should be given. If the dog proves responsive, you may attempt extending his legs to the "down" position—leaving the muzzle on, of course. Daily reinforcement of the training method will soon yield the desired results. The keys to remember are: patience, persistence, and praise.

"Problems with the Barking Dog" and "Aggressive Behavior and Dominance" are extracts from the veterinary monograph *Canine Behavior* (a compilation of columns from *Canine Practice,* a journal published by Veterinary Practice Publishing Company).

### PROBLEMS WITH THE BARKING DOG

One of the most frequent complaints about canine behavior is barking. Aside from the biting dog, the barking dog is probably the pet peeve of many non-dog owners. I know of at least one city in which owners of dogs that bark excessively, and for which there are complaints on file, are required to take steps to eliminate the barking.

Canine practitioners are drawn into problems with barking when they are asked for their advice in helping an owner come up with a solution or, as a last resort, when they are requested to perform a debarking operation or even euthanasia. In this column I will deal with some of the factors that apparently cause dogs to bark and suggest some corrective approaches.

Barking is, of course, a natural response for many dogs. They have an inherited predisposition to bark as an alarm when other dogs or people approach their territory. Alarm barking makes many dogs valuable as household watchdogs and is not necessarily undesirable behavior. With a different vocal tone and pattern, dogs bark when they are playing with each other. On occasion dogs have a tendency to bark back at other dogs or join in with other barking dogs.

In addition to inherited barking tendencies, dogs can also learn to bark if the barking is followed, at least sometimes,

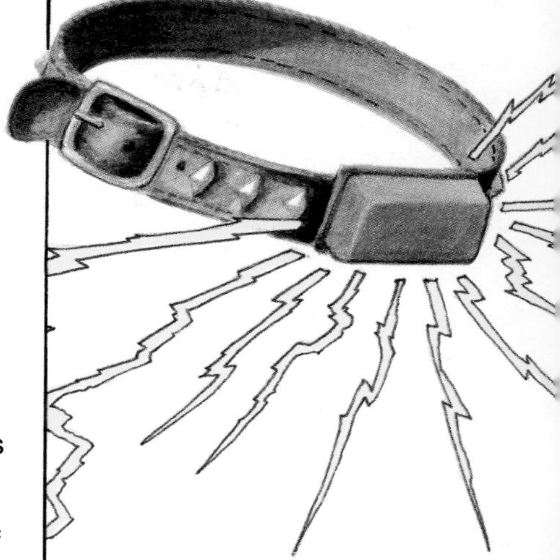

*Only in the most extreme situations may trainers recommend electric-shock collars for correcting a dog's misbehavior.*

*Though jealous by nature, Pekingese can easily be trained to share the affection of their master. Photo by Robert Smith.*

by a reward. Thus dogs may bark when they wish to come in the house or to get out of a kennel. Some dogs are trained to bark upon hearing the command "speak" for a food reward.

One of the first approaches to take when discussing a barking problem is to determine if the behavior is a manifestation of a natural (inherited) tendency or is learned behavior which has been rewarded in the past.

**Can Barking Be Extinguished?** Extinction, as a way of eliminating a behavioral problem, may be considered when it is clear that the behavior has been learned and when one can identify the specific rewarding or reinforcing factors that maintain the behavior.

For example, the dog that barks upon hearing the command "speak" is periodically rewarded with food and praise. If a dog is never, ever given food or praise again when it barks after being told to "speak," it will eventually stop this type of barking. This is the process of extinction and it implies that the behavior must be repeated but never again rewarded.

A more practical example of the possible use of extinction would be in dealing with the dog that apparently barks because, at least occasionally, it is allowed in the house. By not allowing the dog in the house

*Muzzles may prevent biting, but the root cause of biting must be extracted if the dog is to live as a trusted member of the human family.*

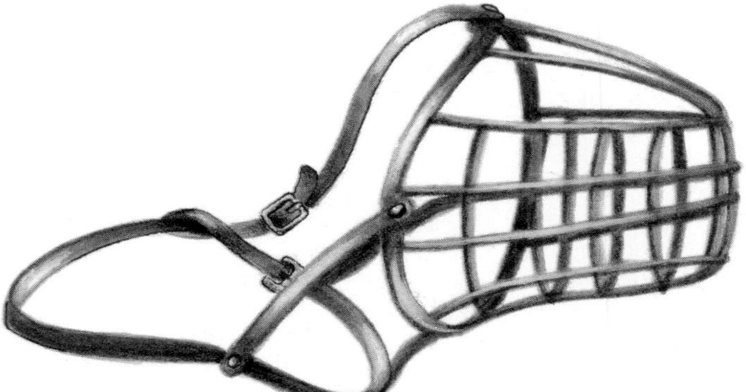

until the barking has become very frequent and loud, the owners may have shaped the barking behavior to that which is the most objectionable. If the dog is never allowed in the house again when barking, the barking should eventually be extinguished—at least theoretically.

**How Should Punishment Be Used?** Sometimes it is not feasible to attempt to extinguish barking even if it seems to be the case that the behavior was learned. This brings up the advisability of punishment. Clients who seek advice in dealing with a barking problem may already have employed some type of punishment such as shouting at the dog or throwing something at it. That this type of punishment is ineffective is attested to by the fact that the client is seeking advice. By shouting at a dog or hitting, a person interferes with what effect the punishment may have on the behavior itself through the arousal of autonomic reactions and escape attempts or submissive responses by the dog.

**The Water Bucket Approach** I am rather impressed by the ingenuity of some dog owners in coming up with ways to punish a dog for barking without being directly involved in administering the punishment. One such

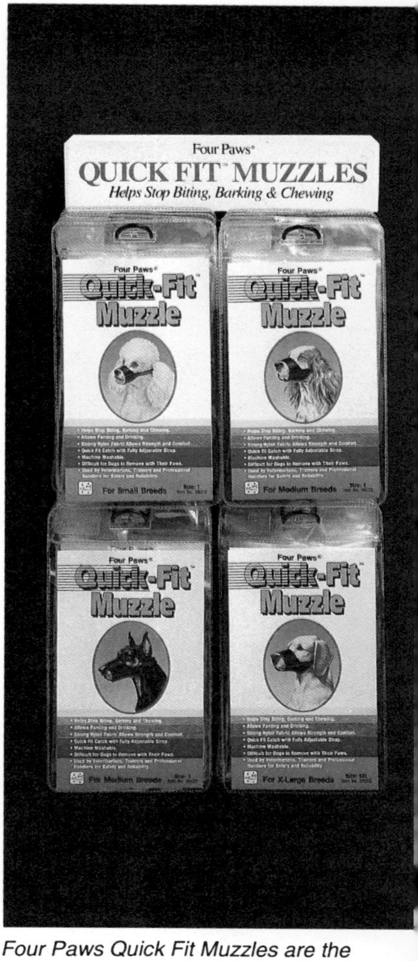


*Four Paws Quick Fit Muzzles are the most comfortable and humane muzzles for dogs. Allow dogs to drink water while wearing the muzzles. They are made of nylon and are completely washable.*

*One fascination of the Pekingese character is that you never quite know exactly what they are thinking. Owner, Elizabeth Nisbet.*

*Pet gates are used to confine a dog to certain areas of the house. The dog must learn to accept any such restrictions and not attempt to overcome them.*

harried dog owner I talked to, who was also a veterinarian, was plagued by his dog's barking in the kennel commencing at about 1:30 a.m. every night. A platform to hold a bucket of water was constructed over the area of the kennel in which the dog usually chose to bark. Through a system of hinges, ropes, and pulleys, a mechanism was devised so that the dog owner could pull a rope from his bedroom window, dumping a bucket of water on the dog when he started to bark. The bucket was suspended such that once it was dumped, it uprighted itself and the owner could fill it again remotely by turning on a garden hose. After two appropriate dunkings, the dog's barking behavior was apparently eliminated.

In advising a client on the type of punishment discussed above, keep in mind one important consideration. From the time the owner is ready to administer punishment for barking, every attempt should be made to punish all undesirable barking from that point on and not to allow excessively long periods of barking to go unpunished. Thus it may be necessary to keep a dog indoors when away unless the dog will be punished for barking when the owner is gone.

**Alternative Responses** Barking dogs are, and probably always will be, one of the enduring problems of dog owners. Barking is relatively effortless, and it is such a natural response for many dogs that it is admittedly hard to eliminate with either punishment or a program of conditioning non-barking. In some instances it may be advisable to forget about eliminating barking and to suggest that the problem be dealt with by changing the circumstances which lead to barking. For example, a dog that barks continuously in the backyard while the owners are away may not bark if left in the house while they are gone. But the problem of keeping the dog in the house may be related to inadequate house training or the

*Four Paws repellents are excellent training aids to keep dogs out of forbidden areas. Use indoors on furniture and rugs; outdoor formula for flowerbeds, shrubs and garbage cans.*

*This pretty Pekingese is owned by Mary Gay.*

dog's shedding hair or climbing onto the furniture. It may be easier to correct these latter behavioral problems than it is to change the barking behavior.

## AGGRESSIVE BEHAVIOR AND DOMINANCE

Aggressiveness can have many causes. Determining what kind of aggression an animal is manifesting is a prerequisite to successful treatment of the behavior. A frequent problem that is presented to the practitioner is one of aggression related to dominance.

Dogs, which are social animals, have a hierarchal system of dominance within their pack. This predisposition to take a dominant or submissive position relative to fellow canines also occurs in relationship to people. Only in unusual situations would a submissive dog threaten a dominant animal, and almost never would it physically assault its superior. The dominant dog, however, frequently threatens submissive individuals to maintain its position. In a household setting, a person may be the object of threats, and when the person backs off, the dog's position is reassured. The aggressive behavior is also reinforced, and when behavior is reinforced it is likely to recur.

*Owners must take an active part in shaping their dog's behavior. Providing a sensible chew device can help alleviate an animal's frustration and thereby eliminate some undersirable behavior. Once a dog has chewed the Gumabone® to this extent, it's time to buy a new one.*

**Case History** The following is a typical case history of a dog presented for aggression stemming from dominance.

Max was a two-year-old intact male Cocker Spaniel. He had been acquired by Mr. Smith, one year prior to his owner's marriage, as a puppy. He liked and was well liked by both Mr. and Mrs. Smith. He frequently solicited and received attention from both people. However, several times over the last few months, Max had snapped at Mrs. Smith and repeatedly growled at her. A detailed anamnesis revealed that such incidents usually occurred in situations where the dog wanted his own way or did not want to be bothered. He would growl if asked to move off a chair or if persistently commanded to do a specific task. He growled if Mrs. Smith came between him and a young female Cocker Spaniel acquired a year ago. He also refused to let Mrs. Smith take anything from his possession. Max never showed any of these aggressive behaviors toward Mr. Smith or strangers. Admittedly he did not have much opportunity to demonstrate such behaviors toward strangers. A description of the dog's body and facial postures and circumstances under which the aggression occurred did not indicate that this was a case of fear-induced aggression, but rather one of assertion of dominance.

*Treats can be effective in shaping behavior and establishing a rapport with your pet.*

Mrs. Smith's reaction to the aggression was always to retreat, and, hence, the dog was rewarded for his assertiveness. She had never physically disciplined the dog and was afraid to do so. To encourage her to physically take control of the dog would likely have resulted in her being bitten. The dominance-submissive

*The Pekingese is a hardy little dog and has stamina much greater than his size. Be sure to keep your Peke away from any poisonous plants when romping outside.*

*While crates may be used principally for sleeping and traveling, some owners might opt to employ a crate for disciplining a dog, rather like sending a naughty child to his room.*

relationship had to be reversed in a more subtle manner.

**Instructions to Client** Mrs. Smith was instructed to avoid all situations which might evoke any aggressive signs from Max. This was to prevent any further reinforcement of his growling and threats.

Both she and her husband were not to indiscriminately pet or show affection towards the dog. For the time being, if Max solicited attention from Mr. Smith, he was to ignore the dog. Mrs. Smith was to take advantage of Max's desire for attention by giving him a command which he had to obey before she praised and petted him. She was also to take advantage of high motivation levels for other activities whenever such situations arose. Max had to obey a command before she gave him anything—

before she petted him, before she let him out or in, etc.

Mrs. Smith also was to assume total care of the dog and become "the source of all good things in life" for Max. She was to feed him, take him on walks, play with him, etc.

Mrs. Smith also spent 5–10 minutes a day teaching Max simple parlor tricks and obedience responses for coveted food rewards as well as praise. These were entirely fun and play sessions—but within a few days the dog had acquired the habit of quickly responding to commands. And this habit transferred over to the non-game situations.

**Results** Within a few weeks, Max had ceased to growl and threaten Mrs. Smith in situations that he previously had. He would move out of her way or lie quietly when she would pass by him. She could order him off the furniture and handle the female Cocker Spaniel without eliciting threats from Max.

Mrs. Smith still felt that she would not be able to take the objects from Max's possession. Additional instructions were given to her. She then began placing a series of objects at progressively closer distances to the dog while the dog was in a sit-stay position. After she placed the object on the floor for a short time, she would pick it up. If the dog was still in a sit-stay (which it always was), he received a reward of cheese and verbal praise. Eventually the objects were to be placed and removed from directly in front of the dog. At first she was to use objects that the dog did not care much about and then progressively use more coveted items. This was what she was supposed to do, but before she actually had completed the program she called in excitedly to report that she had taken a piece of stolen food and a household ornament from Max's mouth. And he didn't even object! She said she had calmly told Max to sit. He did. He was so used to doing so, in the game and other situations, that the response was now automatic. She walked over, removed the item from his mouth, and praised him.

Mrs. Smith did resume the systematic presentation of objects and put the dog on an intermittent schedule of food and praise reinforcement during the practice sessions. Mr. Smith again began interacting with Max.

A progress check six months later indicated Max was still an obedient dog and had definitely assumed a submissive position relative to both of his owners. The dominance hierarchy between Max and Mrs. Smith had been reversed *without resorting to any physical punishment.* Mrs. Smith was instructed to reinforce her dominance position by frequently giving Max a command and reinforcing him for the appropriate response.

**Summary** The essential elements in treatment of such cases are as follows. First, of course, there must be a correct diagnosis of what kind of aggressive behavior is occurring. During the course of treatment, the submissive person(s) should avoid all situations that might evoke an aggressive attitude by the dog. All other family members should totally ignore the dog during the treatment interim. The person most dominated by the dog should take over complete care of the dog in addition to spending 5–10 minutes a day teaching the dog tricks or simple obedience commands (sit-stay is a useful one to gain control of the dog in subsequent circumstances). These should be fun-and-games situations. Food rewards are highly recommended in addition to simple praise.

The person submissive to the dog should take the opportunity to give the dog a command, which must be obeyed, before doing anything pleasant for the dog.

*Four Paws offers Bitter Lime in two ways. A pump spray to stop fur biting and a gel to stop chewing of furniture. Both are safe and non-toxic.*

It must be emphasized to the owner that no guarantee can be made that the dog will never threaten or be aggressive again. What is being done, as with all other aggression cases, is an attempt to reduce the likelihood, incidence, and intensity of occurrence of the aggressive behavior.

*Old discardable shoes should not be included in the dog's toy box. Such items are dangerous to a puppy or an adult dog.*

**DESTRUCTIVE TENDENCIES**

It is ironical but true that a dog's destructive behavior in the home may be proof of his love for his owner. He may be trying to get more attention from his owner or, in other cases, may be expressing his frustration at his owner's absence. An abundance of unused energy may also contribute to a dog's destructive behavior, and therefore the owner should ensure that his dog has, at least, twenty minutes of vigorous exercise a day.

As a dog's destructive tendencies may stem from his desire to get more attention from his owner, the latter should devote specific periods each day to his dog when he is actively interacting with him. Such a period should contain practice obedience techniques during which the owner can reward the dog with his favorite food as well as praise and affection.

Planned departure conditioning is one specific technique which has been used to solve the problem of destructive tendencies in a puppy. It eventually ensures the dog's good behavior during the owner's absence. A series of short departures, which are identical to real departures, should condition the dog to behave well in the owner's absence. How is this to be achieved? Initially, the departures are so short (2–5 minutes) that the dog has no opportunity to be destructive.

The dog is always rewarded for having been good when the owner returns. Gradually the duration of the departures is increased. The departure time is also varied so that the dog does not know when the owner is going to return. Since a different kind of behavior is now expected, it is best if a new stimulus or "atmosphere" is introduced into the training sessions to permit the dog to distinguish these departures as different from previous departures when he was destructive.

This new stimulus could be the sound of the radio or television. The association which the dog will develop is that whenever the "signal" or "stimulus" is on, the owner will return in an unknown period of time and, if the dog has not been destructive, he will be rewarded. As with the daily owner-dog interaction, the food reward is especially useful.

If the dog misbehaves during his owner's absence, the owner should speak sternly to him and isolate him from social contact for at least thirty minutes. (Puppies hate to be ignored.) Then the owner should conduct another departure of a shorter time and generously reward good behavior when he returns. The owner should progress slowly enough in the program so that once the departure has been initiated, the dog is never given an opportunity to make a mistake.

If planned departures are working satisfactorily, the departure time may gradually be extended to several hours. To reduce the dog's anxiety when left alone, he should be given a "safety valve" such as the indestructible Nylabone® to play with and chew on.

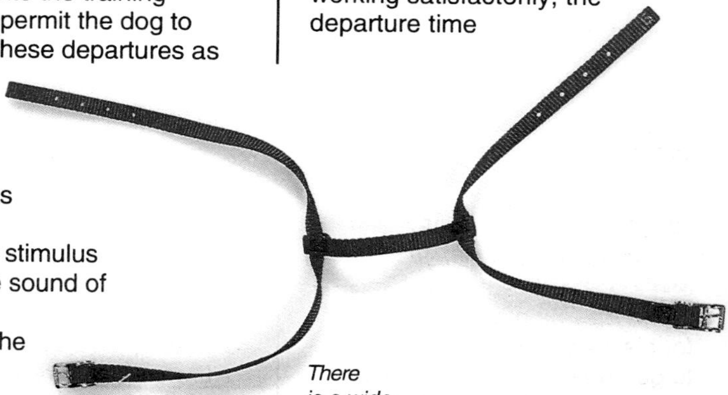

*There is a wide variety of collars and harnesses available to the dog owner. Talk with your pet shop proprietor to determine which one best satisfies your needs.*

From the moment you purchase your puppy, the most important person in both your lives becomes your veterinarian. His professional advice and treatment will ensure the good health of your pet. The vet is the first person to call when illness or accidents occur. Do *not* try to be your own veterinarian or apply human remedies to canine diseases. However, just as you would keep a first aid kit handy for minor injuries sustained by members of your family at home, so you should keep a similar kit prepared for your pet.

First aid for your dog would consist of stopping any bleeding, cleaning the wound, and preventing infection. Thus your kit might contain medicated powder, gauze bandages, and adhesive tape to be used in case of cuts. If the cut is deep and bleeding profusely, the bandage should be applied very tightly to help in the formation of a clot. A tight bandage should not be kept in place longer than necessary, so take your pet to the veterinarian immediately.

Walking or running on a cut pad prevents the cut from healing. Proper suturing of the cut and regular changing of the bandages should have your pet's wound healed in a week to ten

*Bandaging a minor cut on the paw pad is one of many basic first-aid techniques that the dog owner should learn. Thoroughly clean the injury with peroxide and apply an antibiotic. Then place the injured pad in sterile gauze, secure with first-aid tape, and replace daily.*

days. A minor cut should be covered with a light bandage, for you want as much air as possible to reach the wound. Do not apply wads of cotton to a wound, as they will stick to the area and may cause contamination.

You should also keep some hydrogen peroxide available, as it is useful in cleaning wounds and is also one of the best and simplest emetics known. Cotton applicator swabs are useful for applying ointment or removing debris from the eyes. A pair of tweezers should also be kept handy for removing foreign bodies from the dog's neck, head or body.

Nearly everything a dog might contract in the way of sickness has basically the same set of symptoms: loss of appetite, diarrhea, dull eyes, dull coat, warm and/or runny nose, and a high temperature. Therefore, it is most important to take his temperature at the first sign of illness. To do this, you will need a rectal thermometer which should be lubricated with petroleum jelly. Carefully insert it into the rectum, holding it in place for at least two minutes. It must be held firmly; otherwise there is the danger of its being sucked up into the rectum or slipping out, thus giving an inaccurate reading. The normal temperature for a dog is between 101° and 102.5°F. If your pet is seriously ill or injured in an accident, your veterinarian will advise you what to do before he arrives.

*Four Paws Crystal Eye is a safe product for the removal of ugly tear stains.*

## SWALLOWING FOREIGN OBJECTS

Most of us have had experience with a child swallowing a foreign object. Usually it is a small coin; occasionally it may be a fruit pit or something more dangerous. Dogs, *as a general rule,* will not swallow anything which isn't edible. There are, however, many dogs that swallow pebbles or small shiny objects such as pins, coins, and bits of cloth and plastic. This is especially true of dogs that are offered so-called "chew toys."

Chew toys are available in many sizes, shapes, colors and materials. Some even have whistles which sound when the dog's owner plays with it or when the dog chomps on it quickly. Most dogs attack the whistle first, doing everything possible to make it stop squeaking. Obviously, if the whistle is made of metal, a dog

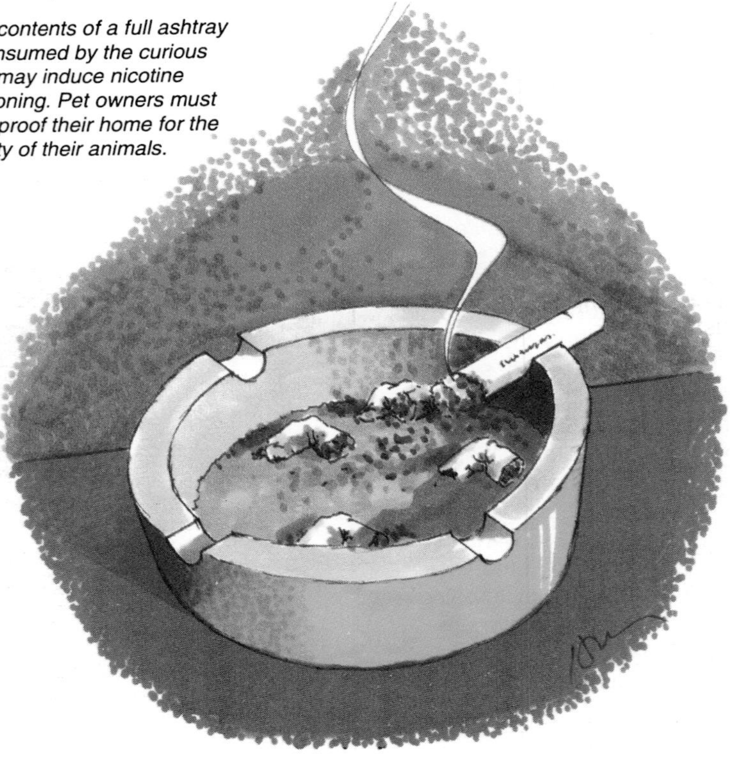

*The contents of a full ashtray if consumed by the curious dog may induce nicotine poisoning. Pet owners must dog-proof their home for the safety of their animals.*

*When emergencies occur, being prepared pays off. A first-aid kit should be accessible and always well stocked with medical accessories and supplies.*

can injure its mouth, teeth, or tongue. Therefore, *never* buy a "squeak toy" made with a metal whistle.

Other chew toys are made of vinyl, a cheap plastic which is soft to the touch and pliable. Most of the cute little toys that are figures of animals or people are made of this cheap plastic. They are sometimes hand-painted in countries where the cost of such labor is low. Not only is the paint used dangerous to dogs, because of the lead content, but the vinyl tears easily and is usually destroyed by the dog during the first hour. Small bits of vinyl may be ingested and cause blockage of the intestines. You are, therefore, reminded of these things before you buy anything vinyl for your dog!

Very inexpensive dog toys, usually found in supermarkets and other low-price venues, may be made of polyethylene. These are to be avoided completely, as this cheap plastic is, for some odd reason, attractive to dogs. Dogs destroy the toy in minutes and sometimes swallow the indigestible bits and pieces that come off. Most pet shops carry only safe toys.

## WHAT TOYS ARE SAFE FOR DOGS?

**Hard Rubber** Toys made of hard rubber are usually safe for dogs, providing the toy is made of 100% hard rubber and not a compound of rubber and other materials. The rubber must be "virgin" and not re-ground from old tires, tubes, and other scrap rubber products. The main problem with rubber, even 100% virgin rubber, is that it oxidizes quickly, especially when subjected to the ultraviolet rays of the sun and a dog's saliva. The rubber then tends to be brittle, to crack, to dust off, and to be extremely dangerous to dogs that like swallowing things.

**Nylon Toys** Toys made of nylon could well be the safest of all toys, *providing the nylon is annealed*. Nylon that is not annealed is very fragile, and if you smash it against a hard surface, it might shatter like glass. The same is true when the weather is cold and the nylon drops below freezing. Thus far there is only one line of dog toys that is made of annealed virgin nylon—Nylabone®. These toys not only are annealed but they are flavored and scented. The flavors and scents, such as hambone, are undetectable by humans, but dogs seem to find them attractive.

Some nylon bones have the

*The Plaque Attacker® is a Dental Ball™, not just a plaything, designed to reduce plaque and tartar by use of its revolutionary "dental tips."*

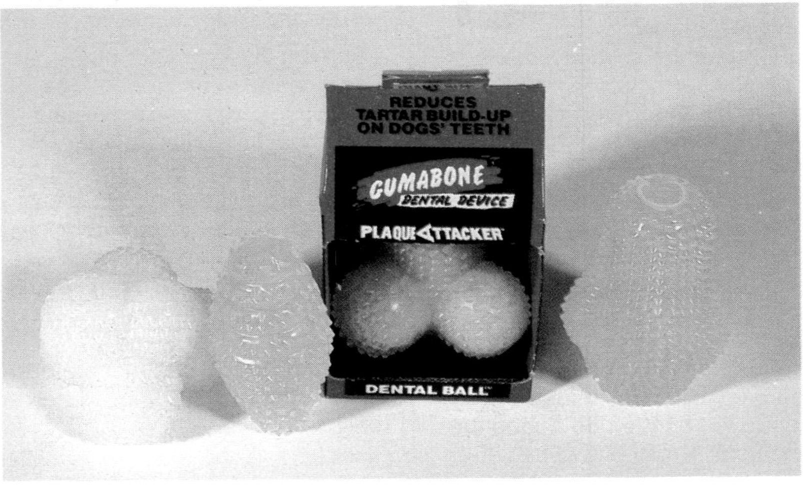

flavor sprayed on them or molded into them. These cheaper bones are easy to detect—just smell them. If you discern an odor, you know they are poorly made. The main problem with the nylon toys that have an odor is that they are not annealed and they "smell up" the house or car. The dog's saliva dilutes the odor of the bone, and when he drops it on your rug, this odor attaches itself to the rug and is quite difficult to remove.

*The Puppy Bone® by Nylabone® is multi-purpose: designed for teething, chew-pacification, teeth-cleaning and the elimination of behavioral problems before they become habitual.*

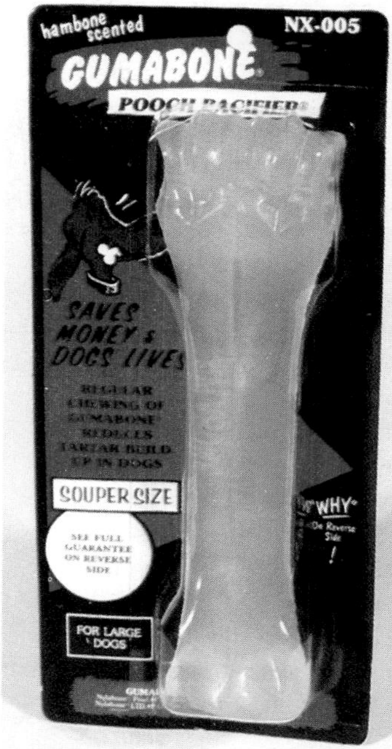


*Gumabone® is available in different sizes and shapes. These are probably the most popular of all chew toys because dogs love them.*

Annealed nylon may be the best there is, but it is not 100% safe. The Nylabone® dog chews are really meant to be Pooch Pacifiers®. This trade name indicates the effect intended for the dog, which is to relieve the tension in your excited puppy or anxious adult dog. Instead of chewing up the furniture or some other object, he chews up his Nylabone® instead. Many dogs ignore the Nylabone® for weeks, suddenly attacking it when they have to relieve their doggie tensions.

The Nylabone® is designed for the most aggressive chewers. Even so, owners should be wary that some dogs may have jaws strong enough to chomp off a piece of Nylabone®, but this is extremely rare. *One word of caution:* the Nylabone® should be replaced when the dog has chewed down the knuckle. Most dogs slowly scrape off small slivers of nylon which pass harmlessly through their digestive tract. The resultant frizzled bone actually becomes a toothbrush.

One of the great characteristics of nylon bones is that they can be boiled and sterilized. If a dog loses interest in his Nylabone®, or it is too hard for him to chew due to his age and the condition of his teeth, you can cook it in some chicken or beef broth, allowing it to boil for 30 minutes. Let it cool down normally. It will then be perfectly sterile and re-flavored for the next dog. *Don't try this with plastic bones, as they will melt and ruin your pot.*

**Polyurethane Toys** Because polyurethane bones such as the Gumabone® are constructed of

*Plaque Attacker™ Dental Bones from Gumabone® are designed for maximum tartar reduction for the aggressive chewer.*

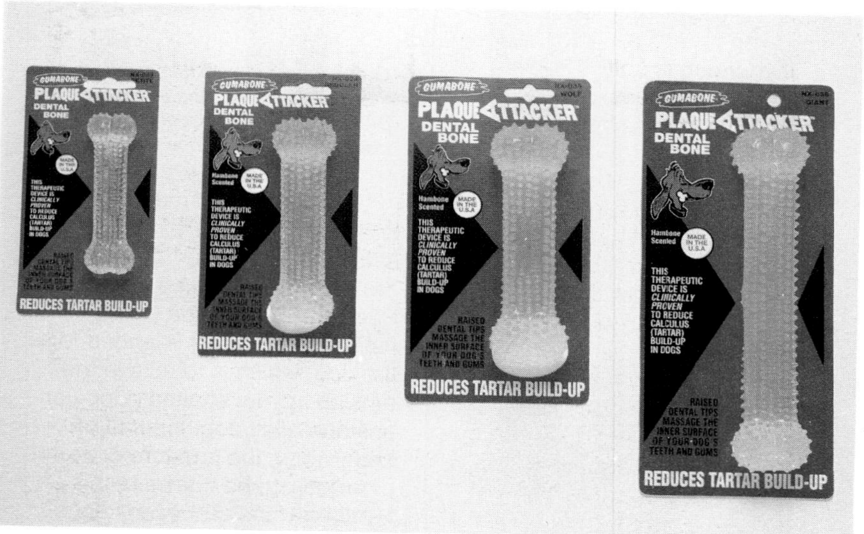

the strongest *flexible* materials known, some dogs (and their owners) actually prefer them to the traditional nylon bones. There are several brands on the market: ignore the ones which have scents that you can discern. Some of the scented polyurethane bones have an unbearable odor after the scent has rubbed off the bone and onto your rug or car seat. Again, look for the better-quality polyurethane toy. Gumabone® is a flexible material, the same as used for making artificial hearts and the bumpers on automobiles, thus it is strong and stable. It is not as strong as Nylabone®, but many dogs like it because it is soft.

If your dog is soft-mouthed and a less aggressive, more playful chewer, he will love the great taste and fun feel of the Gumabone® products.

The most popular of the Gumabone® products made in polyurethane are the tug toys, knots, balls, and Frisbee® flying discs. These items are almost clear in color, have the decided advantage of lasting a long time, and are useful in providing exercise for both a dog and his master or mistress.

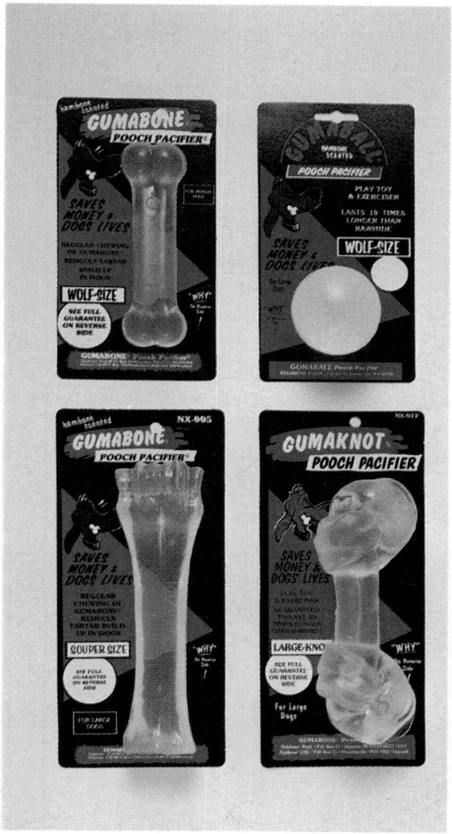

*Made of a more flexible material than nylon, Gumabone® devices often are more appealling to dogs.*

Gumabone® has also introduced new spiral-shaped dental devices under the name Plaque Attacker®. These unique products are fast becoming standards for all aggressive chewers. The Plaque Attacker Dental Device® comes in four fun sizes and each is designed to maximize gum and teeth massage through its upraised "dental tips," which pimple the surface of the toy. Similarly, the Plaque Attacker Dental Ball® ensures a reduction in plaque and tartar. This one-of-a-kind product provides hours of fun for a dog. It bounces erratically and proves to be the most exciting of all polyurethane toys. All Plaque Attacker® products are patented and scented with hambone to make them even more enticing for the dog. Clinical findings

*The Plaque Attacker™ Dental Ball® is a unique and challenging toy for dogs big and small.*

support the assertion that a significant reduction in calculus accompanies use of the Gumbone® products.

Whatever dog toy you buy, be sure it is high quality. Pet shops and certain supermarkets, as a rule, always carry the better-quality toys. Of course there may be exceptions, but you are best advised to ask your local pet shop operator—or even your veterinarian—what toys are suitable for *your* dog.

In conclusion, if your dog is a swallower of foreign objects, don't give him anything cheap to chew on. If he swallows a coin, you can hardly blame the Treasury! Unless your dog is carefully supervised, use only the largest size Nylabone® and Gumabone®, and replace them as soon as the dog chews down the knuckles. *Do not let the dog take the Nylabone® outdoors.* First of all he can hide and bury it, digging it up when his tensions rise. Then, too, all nylon becomes more brittle when it freezes, even Nylabone®.

## IF YOUR PET SWALLOWS POISON

A poisoned dog must be treated instantly; any delay could cause his death. Different poisons act in different ways and require different treatments. If you know the dog has swallowed an acid, alkali, gasoline, or kerosene, do not induce vomiting. Give milk to dilute the poison and rush him to the vet. If you can find the bottle or container of poison, check the label to see if there is a recommended antidote. If not, try to induce vomiting by giving him a mixture of hydrogen peroxide and water. Mix the regular drugstore strength of hydrogen peroxide (3%) with an equal part of water, but do not attempt to pour it down your dog's throat, as that could cause inhalation pneumonia. Instead, simply pull the dog's lips away from the side of his mouth, making a pocket for depositing the liquid. Use at least a tablespoonful of the mixture for every ten pounds of your dog's weight. He will vomit in about two minutes. When his stomach has settled, give him a teaspoonful of Epsom salts in a little water to empty the intestine quickly. The hydrogen peroxide, on ingestion, becomes oxygen and water and is harmless to your dog; it is the best antidote for phosphorus, which is often used in rat poisons. After you have administered this emergency treatment to your pet and his stomach and bowels have been emptied, rush him to your veterinarian for further care.

*Four Paws offers three pleasantly scented colognes that can be used in between baths to freshen up pets.*

**DANGER IN THE HOME**

There are numerous household products that can prove fatal if ingested by your pet. These include rat poison,

*Wasps can be harmful to dogs and humans alike. Paper wasps often build their nests close to the ground, where a dog may happen to visit.*

antifreeze, boric acid, hand soap, detergents, insecticides, mothballs, household cleansers, bleaches, de-icers, polishes and disinfectants, paint and varnish removers, acetone, turpentine, and even health and beauty aids if ingested in large enough quantities. A word to the wise should be sufficient: what you would keep locked away from your two-year-old child should also be kept hidden from your pet.

There is another danger lurking within the home among the household plants, which are almost all poisonous, even if swallowed in small quantities. There are hundreds of poisonous plants around us, among which are: ivy leaves, cyclamen, lily of the valley, rhododendrons, tulip bulbs, azalea, wisteria, poinsettia leaves, mistletoe, daffodils, delphiniums, foxglove leaves, the jimson weed—we cannot name them all. Rhubarb leaves, for example, either raw or cooked, can cause death or violent convulsions. Peach, elderberry, and cherry trees can cause cyanide poisoning if their bark is consumed.

There are also many insects that can be poisonous to dogs

such as spiders, bees, wasps, and some flies. A few toads and frogs exude a fluid that can make a dog foam at the mouth—and even kill him—if he bites too hard!

There have been cases of dogs suffering nicotine poisoning by consuming the contents of full ashtrays which thoughtless smokers have left on the coffee table. Also, do not leave nails, staples, pins, or other sharp objects lying around. Likewise, don't let your puppy play with plastic bags which could suffocate him. Unplug, remove, or cover any electrical cords or wires near your dog. Chewing live wires could lead to severe mouth burns or death. Remember that an ounce of prevention is worth a pound of cure: keep all potentially dangerous objects out of your pet's reach.

**VEHICLE TRAVEL SAFETY**

A dog should never be left alone in a car. It takes only a few minutes for the heat to become unbearable in the summer, and to drop to freezing in the winter.

A dog traveling in a car or truck should be well behaved. An undisciplined dog can be deadly in a moving vehicle. The dog should be trained to lie on the back seat of the vehicle. Allowing your dog to stick its head out of

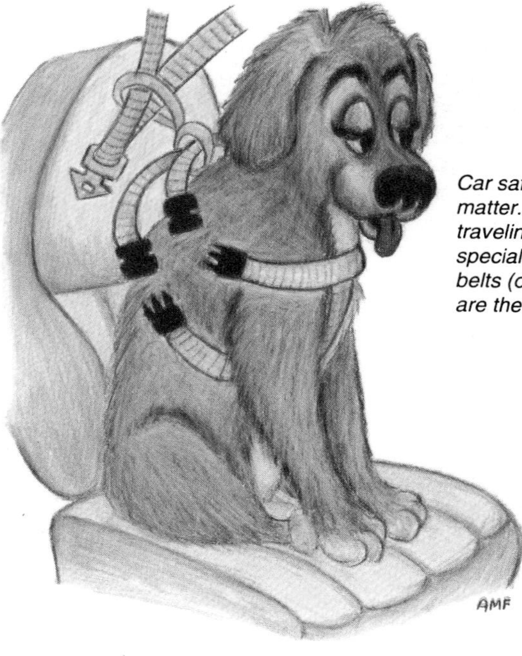


*Car safety is a serious matter. When a dog is traveling by auto, specially designed seat belts (or the dog's crate) are the safest route.*

*Four Paws Pet Safety Sitter is designed to protect pets from injury by securing them in place and preventing them from disturbing drivers and passengers.*

the window is unwise. The dog may jump or it may get something in its eye. Some manufacturers sell seat belts and car seats designed for dogs.

Traveling with your dog in the back of your pick-up truck is an unacceptable notion and dangerous to all involved.

## PROTECT YOURSELF FIRST

In almost all first aid situations, the dog is in pain. He may indeed be in shock and not appear to be suffering, until you move him. Then he may bite your hand or resist being helped at all. So if you want to help your dog, help yourself first by tying his mouth closed. To do this, use a piece of strong cloth four inches wide and three feet long, depending on the size of the dog. Make a loop in the middle of the strip and slip it over his nose with the knot under his chin and over the bony part of his nose. Pull it tight and bring the ends back around his head behind the ears and tie it tightly, ending with a bow knot for quick, easy release. Now you can handle the dog safely. As a dog perspires through his tongue, do not leave the "emergency muzzle" on any longer than necessary.

## ADMINISTERING MEDICINE

When you are giving liquid medicine to your dog, it is a good idea to pull the lips away from the side of the mouth, form a lip pocket, and let the liquid trickle past the tongue. Remain at his side, never in front of the dog, as he may cough and spray you with the liquid. Moreover, you must never pour liquid medicine while the victim's tongue is drawn out, as inhalation pneumonia could be the disastrous result.

Medicine in pill form is best administered by forcing the dog's mouth open, holding his head back, and placing the capsule as far back on his tongue as you can reach. To do this: put the palm of your hand over the dog's muzzle (his foreface) with your fingers on one side of his jaw, your thumb on the other. Press his lips hard against his teeth while using your other hand to pull down his lower jaw. With your two fingers, try to put the pill as far back on the dog's tongue as you can reach. Keep his mouth and nostrils closed and he should be forced to swallow the medicine. As the dog will not be feeling well, stroke his neck to comfort him and to help him swallow his medicine more easily. Do keep an eye on him for a few moments afterward, however, to make certain that he does not spit it out.

## IN CASE OF AN ACCIDENT

It is often difficult for you to assess the dog's injuries after a road accident. He may appear normal, but there might be

*Choose from a variety of ear care products from Four Paws from cleaners to remedies for proper ear hygiene.*

internal hemorrhaging. A vital organ could be damaged or ribs broken. Keep the dog as quiet and warm as possible; cover him with blankets or your coat to let his own body heat build up. Signs of shock are a rapid and weak pulse, glassy-eyed appearance, subnormal temperature, and slow capillary refill time. To determine the last symptom, press firmly against the dog's gums until they turn white. Release and count the number of seconds until the gums return to their normal color. If it is more than 2–3 seconds, the dog may be going into shock. Failure to return to the reddish pink color indicates that the dog may be in serious trouble and needs immediate assistance.

If artificial respiration is required, first open the dog's mouth and check for obstructions; extend his tongue and examine the pharynx. Clear his mouth of mucus and blood and hold the mouth slightly open. Mouth-to-mouth resuscitation involves holding the dog's tongue to the bottom of his mouth with one hand and sealing his nostrils with the other while you blow into his mouth. Watch for his chest to rise with each inflation. Repeat every 5–6 seconds, the equivalent of 10–12 breaths a minute.

If the veterinarian cannot come to you, try to improvise a stretcher to take the dog to him. To carry a puppy, wrap him in a blanket that has been folded into several thicknesses. If he is in shock, it is better to pick him up by holding one hand under his chest, the other under the hindquarters. This will keep him stretched out.

It is always better to roll an injured dog than to try and lift him. If you find him lying beside the road after a car accident, apply a muzzle even if you have to use someone's necktie to make one. Send someone for a blanket and roll him gently onto it. Two people, one on each side, can make a stretcher out of the blanket and move the dog easily.

If no blanket is available and the injured dog must be moved, try to keep him as flat as possible. So many dogs' backs are broken in car accidents that one must first consider that possibility. However, if he can move his hind legs or tail, his spine is probably not broken. Get medical assistance for him immediately.

It should be mentioned that unfortunate car accidents, which can maim or kill your dog, can be avoided if he is confined at all times either indoors or, if out-of-doors, in a fenced-in yard or some other protective enclosure. *Never* allow your dog to roam free; even a well-trained dog may, for some unknown reason,

| VACCINATION SCHEDULE | |
|---|---|
| **Age** | **Vaccination** |
| 6-8 weeks | Initial canine distemper, canine hepatitis, tracheobronchitis, canine parvovirus, as well as initial leptospirosis vaccination. |
| 10-12 weeks | Second vaccination for all given at 6-8 weeks. Initial rabies and initial Lyme disease to be given at this time. |
| 14-16 weeks | Third vaccination for all given at 6-8 and 10-12 weeks.Re-vaccinate annually, hereafter. Second rabies and second Lyme disease to be given at this time, and then re-vaccinated annually. |

*Vaccination schedules should be confirmed with your vet.*

dart into the street—and the result could be tragic.

If you need to walk your dog, leash him first so that he will be protected from moving vehicles.

## PROTECTING YOUR PET

It is important to watch for any tell-tale signs of illness so that you can spare your pet any unnecessary suffering. Your dog's eyes, for example, should normally be bright and alert, so if the haw is bloodshot or partially covers the eye, it may be a sign of illness or irritation. If your dog has matter in the corners of his eyes, bathe them with a mild eye wash; obtain ointment or eye drops from your veterinarian to treat a chronic condition.

If your dog seems to have something wrong with his ears which causes him to scratch at them or shake his head, cautiously probe the ear with a cotton swab. An accumulation of wax will probably work itself out. Dirt or dried blood, however, is indicative of ear mites or infection and should be treated immediately. Sore ears in the summer, due to insect bites, should be washed with mild soap and water, then covered with a soothing ointment and wrapped in gauze if necessary. Keep your

*Mosquitoes are the vectors of disease; although males like this one do not bite, females can transmit heartworm and other diseases to dogs.*

pet away from insects until his ears heal, even if this means confining him indoors.

## INOCULATIONS

Periodic check-ups by your veterinarian throughout your puppy's life are good health insurance. The person from whom your puppy was purchased should tell you what inoculations your puppy has had and when the next visit to the vet is necessary. You must make certain that your puppy has been vaccinated against the following infectious canine diseases: distemper, canine hepatitis, leptospirosis, rabies, parvovirus, and parainfluenza. Annual "boosters" thereafter provide inexpensive protection for your dog against such serious diseases. Puppies should also be checked for worms at an early age.

## DISTEMPER

Young dogs are most susceptible to distemper, although it may affect dogs of all ages. Some signs of the disease are loss of appetite, depression, chills, and fever, as well as a watery discharge from the eyes and nose. Unless treated promptly, the disease goes into advanced stages with infections of the lungs, intestines, and nervous system. Dogs that recover may be impaired with paralysis, convulsions, a twitch, or some other defect, usually spastic in nature. Early inoculations in puppyhood should be followed by an annual booster to help protect against this disease.

## CANINE HEPATITIS

The signs of hepatitis are drowsiness, loss of appetite, high temperature, and great thirst. These signs may be accompanied by swellings of the head, neck, and abdomen. Vomiting may also occur. This disease strikes quickly, and death may occur in only a few hours. An annual booster shot is needed after the initial series of puppy shots.

## LEPTOSPIROSIS

Infection caused by either of two serovars, *canicola* or *copehageni,* is usually begun by the dog's licking substances contaminated by the urine or feces of infected animals. Brown rats are the main carriers of *copehageni.* The signs are weakness, vomiting, and a

*Biting bugs not only have a painful bite but also carry blood parasites.*

yellowish discoloration of the jaws, teeth, and tongue, caused by an inflammation of the kidneys. A veterinarian can administer the bacterins to protect your dog from this disease. The frequency of the doses is determined by the risk factor involved.

**RABIES**

This disease of the dog's central nervous system spreads by infectious saliva, which is transmitted by the bite of an infected animal. Of the two main classes of signs, the first is "furious rabies," in which the dog shows a period of melancholy or depression, then irritation, and finally paralysis. The first period can be from a few hours to several days, and during this time the dog is cross and will change his position often, lose his appetite, begin to lick, and bite or swallow foreign objects. During this phase the dog is spasmodically wild and has impulses to run away. The dog acts fearless and bites everything in sight. If he is caged or confined, he will fight at the bars and possibly break teeth or fracture his jaw. His bark becomes a peculiar howl. In the final stage, the animal's lower jaw becomes paralyzed and

*Heartworm life cycle: a carrier mosquito bites a dog and deposits microfilariae, which travel through the dog's bloodstream, lodging in the heart to reproduce. The carrier dog is later bitten by an uninfected mosquito, which becomes infected, and bites and infects another dog...*

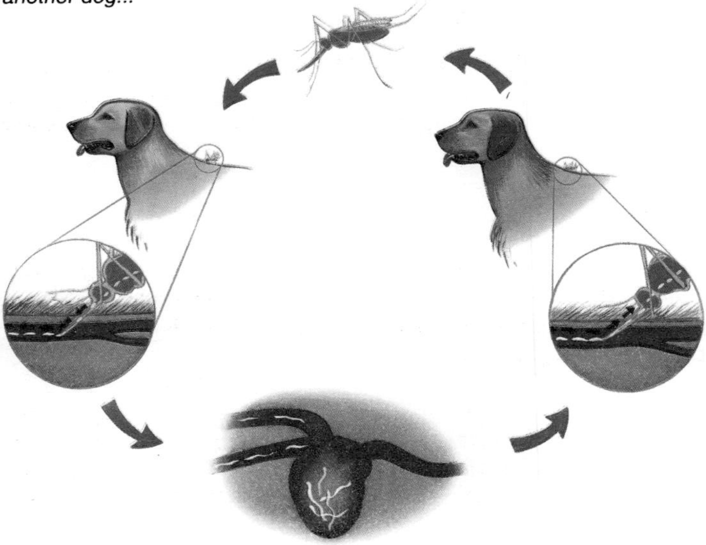

hangs down. He then walks with a stagger, and saliva drips from his mouth. About four to eight days after the onset of paralysis, the dog dies.

The second class of symptoms is referred to as "dumb rabies" and is characterized by the dog's walking in a bearlike manner with his head down. The lower jaw is paralyzed and the dog is unable to bite. It appears as if he has a bone caught in his throat.

If a dog is bitten by a rabid animal, he probably can be saved if he is taken to a veterinarian in time for a series of injections. After the signs appear, however, no cure is possible. The local health department must be notified in the case of a rabid dog, for he is a danger to all who come near him. As with the other shots each year, an annual rabies inoculation is very important. In many areas, the administration of rabies vaccines for dogs is required by law.

## PARVOVIRUS

This relatively new virus is a contagious disease that has spread in almost epidemic proportions throughout certain sections of the United States. It has also appeared in Australia, Canada, and Europe. Canine parvovirus attacks the intestinal tract, white blood cells, and heart muscle. It is believed to spread through dog-to-dog contact, and the specific course of infection seems to come from fecal matter of infected dogs. Overcoming parvovirus is difficult, for it is capable of existing in the environment for many months under varying conditions and temperatures, and it can be transmitted from place to place

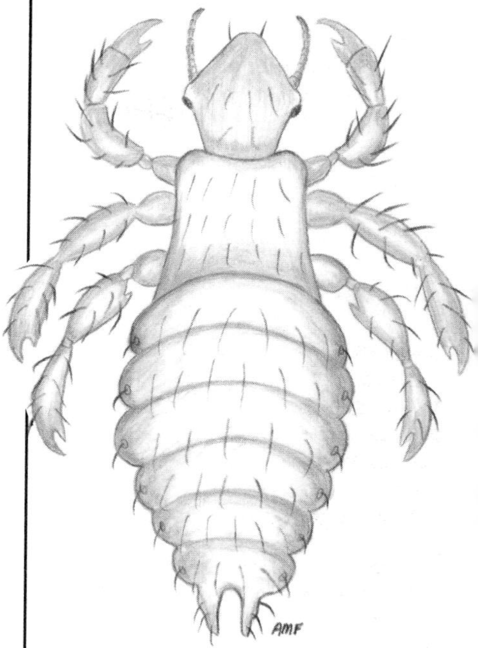


*Lice are not a common problem in dogs and usually only infest dogs that are poorly cared for. Proper care of your dog will prevent lice infestation.*

*Four Paws Protector Flea & Tick Spray offers a quick kill and will repel fleas for up to 14 days. Super Fly Repellent repels flies and mosquitoes, which are known to transmit heartworm.*

on the hair and feet of infected dogs, as well as on the clothes and shoes of people.

Vomiting and severe diarrhea, which will appear within five to seven days after the animal has been exposed to the virus, are the initial signs of this disease. At the onset of illness, feces will be light gray or yellow-gray in color, and the urine might be blood-streaked. Because of the vomiting and severe diarrhea, the dog that has contracted the disease will dehydrate quickly. Depression and loss of appetite, as well as a rise in temperature, can accompany the other symptoms. Death caused by this disease usually occurs within 48 to 72 hours following the appearance of the symptoms. Puppies are hardest hit, and the virus is fatal to 75 percent of puppies that contract it. Death in puppies can be within two days of the onset of the illness.

A series of shots administered by a veterinarian is the best preventive measure for canine parvovirus. It is also important to disinfect the area where the dog is housed by using one part sodium hypochlorite solution (household bleach) to 30 parts of water and to keep the dog from coming into contact with the fecal matter of other dogs.

### LYME DISEASE

Known as a bacterial infection, Lyme disease is transmitted by ticks infected with a spirochete known as *Borrelia burgdorferi.* The disease is most often acquired by the parasitic bite of an infected deer tick, *Ixodes dammini.* While the range of symptoms is broad, common warning signs include: rash beginning at the bite and soon extending in a bullseye-targetlike fashion; chills, fever, lack of balance, lethargy, and stiffness; swelling and pain, especially in the joints, possibly leading to arthritis or arthritic conditions; heart problems, weak limbs, facial paralysis, and lack of tactile sensation.

Concerned dog owners, especially those living in the United States, should contact a veterinarian to discuss Lyme disease. A vaccination has been developed and is routinely administered to puppies twice before the 16th week, and then repeated annually.

**PARAINFLUENZA**

Parainfluenza, or infectious canine tracheobronchitis, is commonly known as "kennel cough." It is highly contagious, affects the upper respiratory system, and is spread through direct or indirect contact with already diseased dogs. It will readily infect dogs of all ages that have not been vaccinated or that were previously infected. While this condition is definitely one of the serious diseases in dogs, it is self-limiting, usually lasting only two to four weeks. The symptoms are high fever and intense, harsh coughing that brings up mucus. As long as

*The fraternity of internal parasites and their eggs: whipworms, hookworms, roundworms and tapeworms.*

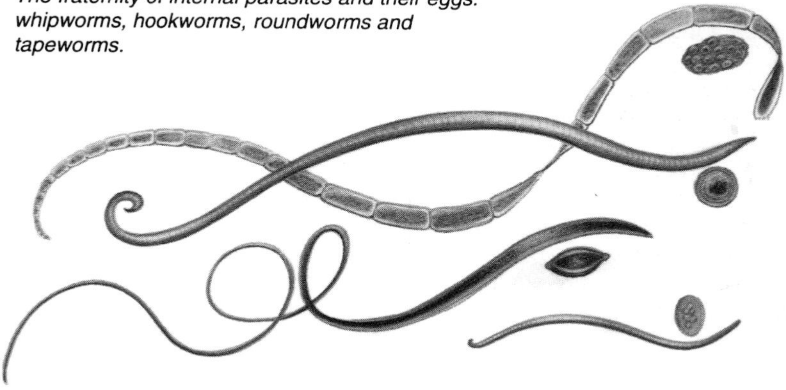

your pet sees your veterinarian immediately, the chances for his complete recovery are excellent.

## EXTERNAL PARASITES

A parasite is an animal that lives in or on an organism of another species, known as the host, without contributing to the well-being of the host. The majority of dogs' skin problems are parasitic in nature and an estimated 90% of puppies are born with parasites.

Ticks can cause serious problems to dogs where the latter have access to woods, fields, and vegetation in which large numbers of native mammals live. Ticks are usually found clinging to vegetation and attach themselves to animals passing by. They have eight legs and a heavy shield or shell-like covering on their upper surface. Only by keeping dogs away from tick-infested areas can ticks on dogs be prevented.

The flea is the single most common cause of skin and coat problems in dogs. There are 11,000 kinds of fleas which can transmit specific disorders like tapeworm and heartworm or transport smaller parasites onto your dog. The common tapeworm, for example, requires the flea as an intermediate host for completion of its life cycle.

A female flea can lay hundreds of eggs and these will become adults in less than three weeks. Depending on the temperature and the amount of moisture, large numbers of fleas can attack dogs. The ears of dogs, in particular, can play host to hundreds of fleas.

Fleas can lurk in crevices and cracks, carpets, and bedding for months, so frequent cleaning of your dog's environment is absolutely essential. If he is infected by other dogs, then have him bathed and "dipped," which means that he will be put into water containing a chemical that kills fleas. Your veterinarian will advise which dip to use, and your dog must be bathed for at least twenty minutes.

## INTERNAL PARASITES

Four common internal parasites that may infect a dog are: roundworms, hookworms, whipworms, and tapeworms. The first three can be diagnosed by laboratory examination of the dog's stool, and tapeworms can be seen in the stool or attached to the hair around the anus. When a veterinarian determines what type of worm or worms are present, he then can advise the best treatment.

Roundworms, the dog's most common intestinal parasite, have a life cycle which permits complete eradication by worming twice, ten days apart. The first worming will remove all adults and the second will destroy all subsequently hatched eggs before they, in turn, can produce more parasites.

A dog in good physical condition is less susceptible to worm infestation than a weak dog. Proper sanitation and a nutritious diet help in preventing worms. One of the best preventive measures is to have clean, dry bedding for the dog, as this diminishes the possibility of reinfection due to flea or tick bites.

Heartworm infestation in dogs is passed by mosquitoes. Dogs with this disease tire easily, have difficulty in breathing, and lose weight despite a hearty appetite. Administration of preventive medicine throughout the spring, summer, and fall months is advised. A veterinarian must first take a blood sample from the dog to test for the presence of the disease, and if the dog is heartworm-free, pills or liquid medicine can be prescribed to protect against any infestation.

## CANINE SENIOR CITIZENS

The processes of aging and gradual degenerative changes start far earlier in a dog than often observed, usually at about seven years of age. Your pet will become less active, will have a poorer appetite with increased thirst, there will be frequent periods of constipation and less than normal passage of urine. His skin and coat might become dull and dry and his hair will become thin and fall out. There is a tendency towards obesity in old age, which should be avoided by maintaining a regular exercise program. Remember, also, that your pet will be less able to cope with extreme heat, cold, fatigue, and change in routine.

There is the possibility of loss or impairment of hearing or eyesight. He may become bad-tempered more often than in the past. Visits to the vet should be more regular. Care of the teeth is also important in the aging dog. Indeed, the mouth can be a barometer of nutritional health. Degenerating gums, heavy tartar on the teeth, loose teeth, and sore lips are common. The worst of all diseases in old age, however, is neglect. Good care in early life will have its effect on your dog's later years; the nutrition and general health care of his first few years can determine his lifespan and the quality of his life. It is worth bearing in mind that the older, compared to the younger, animal needs more protein of good biological value, more vitamins A, B-complex, D and E, more calcium and iron, less fat and fewer carbohydrates.

Quality in the sense of "show quality" is determined by various factors such as the dog's health, physical condition, temperament, ability to move, and appearance. Breeders trying to breed show dogs are attempting to produce animals which come as close as possible to the word description of perfection as set out in the breed standard.

Keep in mind that dog show terminology varies from one place to another and even from one time to another. If you plan to show your dog, it always makes sense to check with your local or national breed club or with the national dog registry for the most complete, most up-to-date information regarding dog show regulations. In Great Britain, for example, match shows are known as limit shows. Age limit also differs, as dogs less than six months old may not be shown in Britain. Additionally, Britain has no point system for dogs, rather the dogs compete for championship certificates (C.C.s). Thus, point shows are known as championship shows in Great Britain.

### MATCH SHOWS

One of the best ways to see if your puppy has championship potential is to attend a match show which is usually organized by the local kennel club or breed specialty club. Such shows provide a useful learning experience for the amateur and they offer you the opportunity to see how well your dog measures up to others being shown. There you can mingle with owners and professional handlers and pick up basic guidelines in showmanship, performance, and procedure. You can learn a great deal merely by closely observing the professional handlers performing in the ring.

The age limit is usually reduced to two months at match shows so that puppies can have four months of training before they compete in the regular shows when they reach six months. This time also helps them to overcome any "crowd nervousness." As class categories are the same as those included at a regular show, much experience can be gained in this informal atmosphere. Entry fees are low and paid at the door.

Before you go to a show, your dog should be trained to gait at a trot beside you, with head up and in a straight line. In the ring you will have to gait

***Facing page:** The most prestigious dog show in America is the Westminster Kennel Club Show held annually in Madison Square Garden, New York City.*

Budweiser
BUD LIGHT
WKC
RING 1
RING 7
WKC
WKC
WKC

around the edge with other dogs and then individually up and down the center runner. In addition, the dog must stand for examination by the judge, who will look at him closely and feel his head and body structure. He should be taught to stand squarely, hind feet slightly back and head up. He must hold the pose when you place his feet, and he must show a lively interest when you "bait" him, i.e., tempt him with a piece of boiled liver or a small squeak toy.

If your puppy receives praise and words of encouragement from the judges and other knowledgeable people, then you can begin to dream of Westminster or Crufts. It is always useful to visit such prestigious shows to see the best examples of all the various breeds.

After you have taken some handling lessons yourself, or employed a professional handler, the next step is participation in the point shows where you can earn points toward your dog's championship.

**POINT SHOWS**

Unlike match shows where your dog was judged on ring behavior, at point shows he will be judged on conformation to his breed standard. It is advisable to write to your national dog registry for information on how to register your dog and apply to dog shows. Below are the names and addresses of registries in the United States, Canada, Great Britain, and Australia.

The American Kennel Club
51 Madison Avenue
New York, NY 10010

The Canadian Kennel Club
111 Eglinton Avenue
East Toronto, Ontario M6S 4V7
Canada

The Kennel Club
1 Clarges Street Piccadilly,
London, W1Y 8AB, England

The Australian Kennel Club
Royal Show Grounds
Ascot Vale, Victoria, Australia.

Your local kennel club can provide you with the names and addresses of the show-giving superintendents (or show secretaries) near you, who will be staging the club's dog show for them, and where you must write for an official entry form. The forms will be mailed in a pamphlet called the "premium list" which will include the names of the judges for each breed, a list of the prizes and trophies, the names and addresses of the show-giving club, where the show will be held, as well as the rules and required procedure. Make certain that you fill in the form clearly and carefully and

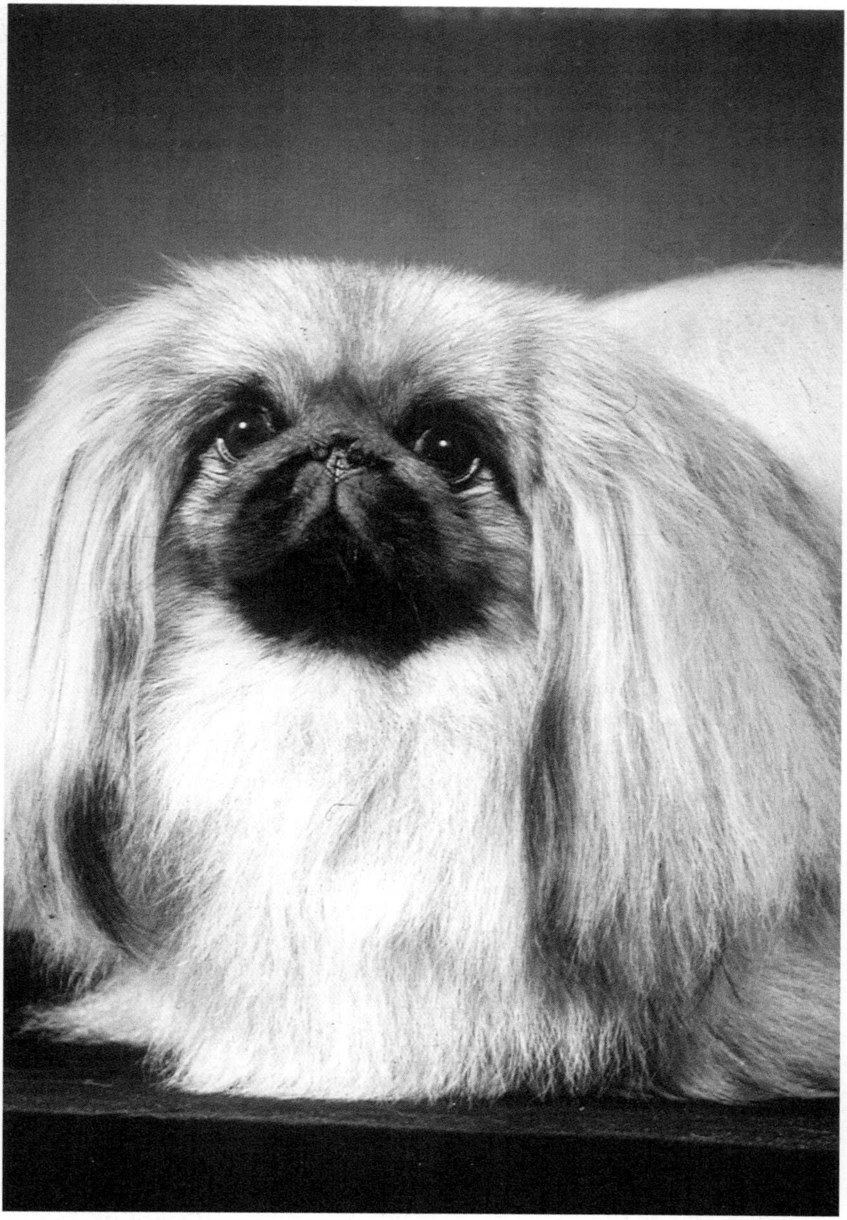

*Ch. St. Aubrey Dragonora of Elsdon, owned by Mrs. Anna E. Snellin. Photo by John Ashbey.*

*Four Paws offers an extensive line of grooming brushes, from slickers to curry brushes to pin brushes. These are sure to suit the grooming needs of every dog.*

mail it in plenty of time.

Before then, however, you will have to decide in which classes your dog should compete. In the United States these are: Puppy, Novice, Bred-by-Exhibitor, American-bred and Open.

*Puppy Classes* are for dogs six months of age and over but under twelve months which are not champions. The age of a dog shall be calculated up to and inclusive of the first day of the show.

The *Novice Class* is for dogs six months of age and over, whelped in the United States or Canada, which have not, prior to the official closing date for entries, won three first prizes in the Novice Class, a first prize in Bred-by-Exhibitor, American-bred or Open Class or one or more points toward championship. In Britain, of course, dogs competing in the Novice Class must have been whelped in Britain.

The *Bred-by-Exhibitor Class*

is for dogs whelped in the U.S.A. or, if individually registered in the American Kennel Club Stud Book, for dogs in Canada that are six months of age and over. They must not be champions (although they may be in Britain), and must be owned wholly or in part by the person or the spouse of the person who was the breeder or one of the breeders of record. Dogs in this class must be handled by an owner or by a member of the immediate family of the owner. (This is not the case, however, in Britain.) Members of an immediate family for this purpose are: husband, wife, father, mother, son, daughter, brother and sister. This class has been referred to as the "breeder's showcase" as it is the one where the breeders can be justly proud of their achievements.

The *American-bred Class* is for all dogs (except champions) six months of age or over, whelped in the U.S.A. by reason of a mating that took place in the U.S.A.

The *Open Class* is for any dog six months of age or over, except in a member specialty club show held only for American-bred dogs, in which

*The Shed 'N Blade is a tool used by groomers and handlers to eliminate dead, unwanted hair and allow for a healthy and vibrant coat.*

***The Pekingese is exhibited in the Toy Group, competing against such breeds as the Pomeranian and the Papillon. Photo by Robert Smith.***

case the class is for American-bred dogs only.

In the United States and Canada, one does not enter the *Winners Class.* One earns the right to compete in it by winning first prize in one of the above classes. Winners Dog and Winners Bitch are the awards which carry points toward championship with them. Also designated by the judge are the Reserve Winners Dog and the Reserve Winners Bitch (in Britain these are designated Reserve C.C. Dog and Reserve C.C. Bitch) but they do not receive any points. This award means simply that the dog or bitch receiving it are standing "in reserve" should the Winners Dog or Winners Bitch be disallowed through any technicality in the official show rules and regulations.

The dog and bitch then compete against each other for Best of Winners, and they also vie with the champions in the Specials Class for Best of Breed and for Best of Opposite Sex to Best of Breed. In Britain, the Reserve C.C. winners compete against each other for Best of Breed, not Best of Winners.

Best of Breed is the highest-placing dog in a given breed, and that winner then represents the particular breed in Group competition. Groups include: Sporting Dogs, Herding Dogs, Hounds, Working Dogs, Terriers, Toys, and Non-sporting Dogs. The judge of each Group selects first, second, third, and fourth place among the Best of Breed winners within specific Groups. First-place winners in each Group then compete for Best in Show.

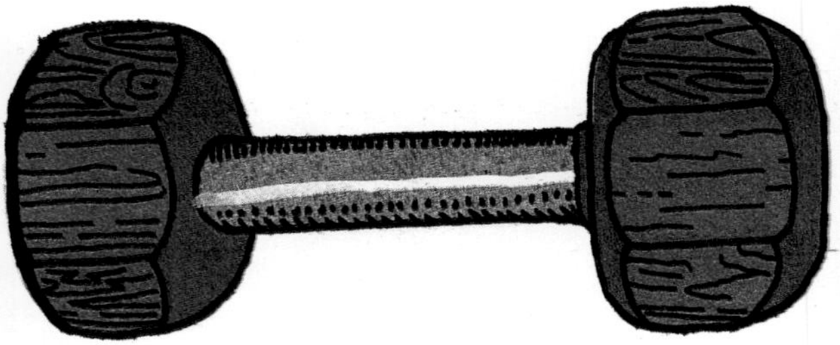

A scale of points is printed in each dog-show catalog, and the number of points awarded in a breed depends on the number of dogs shown in competition. A win of three or more points at a show is called a "major." To attain championship, a dog must win a total of fifteen points under at least three different judges, and included in those fifteen points must be two majors (each under a different judge). A dog that accumulates fifteen points and no majors does not qualify for championship. A dog must win in keen competition. (This is the case in the United States but not in Great Britain. As there is no point system in Britain, it doesn't matter how many dogs are shown in competition. Championship Certificates are awarded at the discretion of the judge, however few dogs are competing.)

## OBEDIENCE AND FIELD TRIALS

It should be mentioned that obedience trials, in which any purebred dog may compete, are often held in conjunction with conformation shows. Dogs are judged on performance rather than on how well they measure up to their breed standard. Many dogs that have already earned their championship in the conformation ring also compete for obedience trial degrees.

*Two training accessories especially common with obedience trial enthusiasts are the hurdle (below) and the dumbbell (facing page). To see dogs performing with these and other field accessories, attend an obedience competition. Remember that training requires consistency and commitment, but the rewards are well worth the effort.*

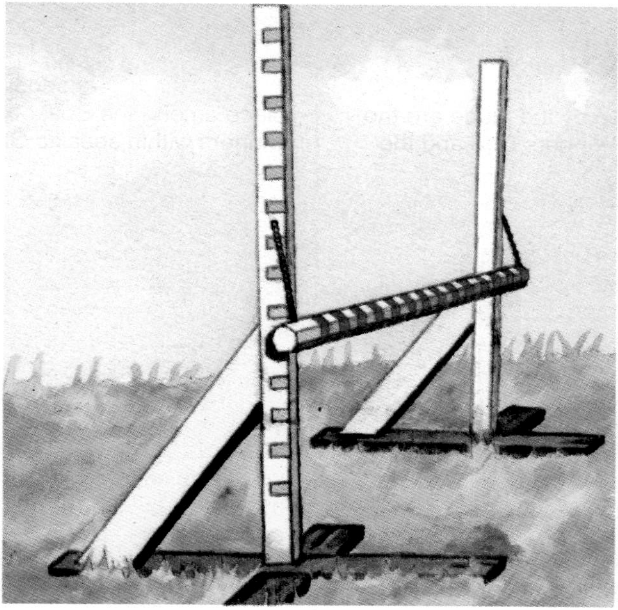

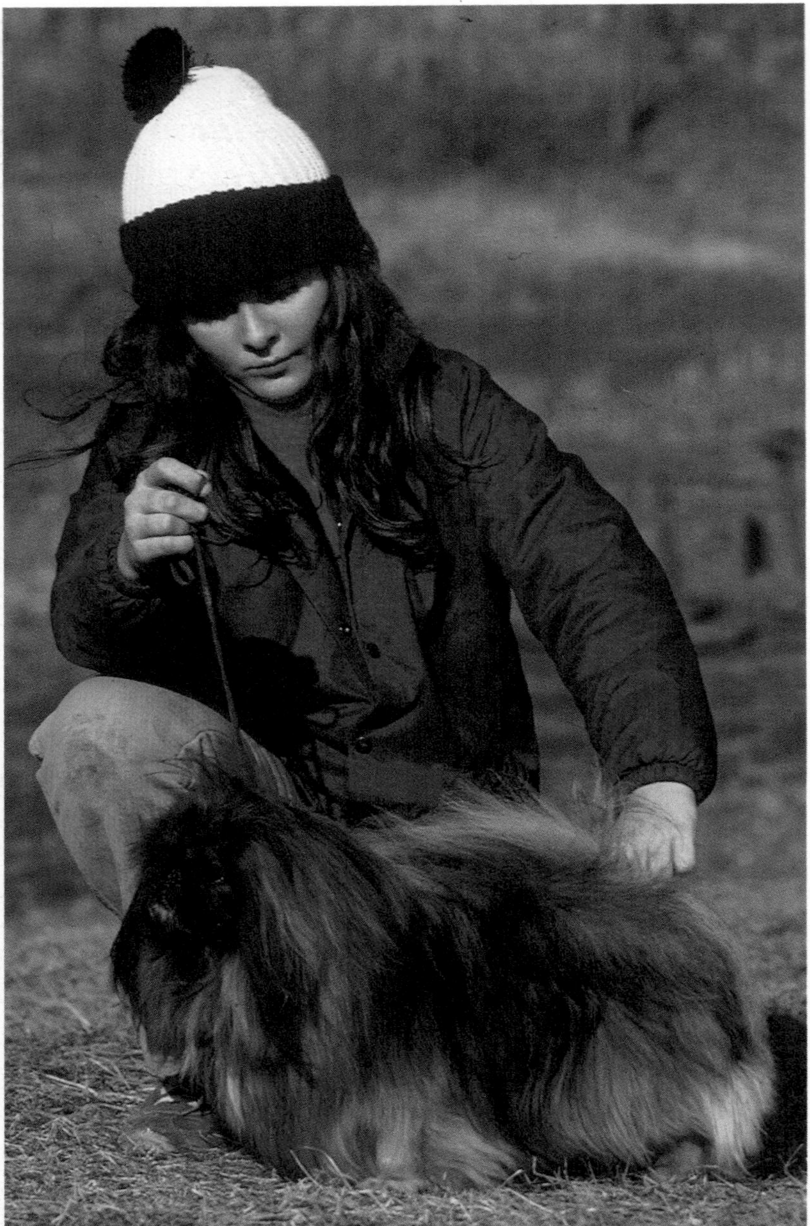

*Practice stacking your Pekingese at home. The tail should be set high; lying well over back to either side with long, profuse, straight feathering.*

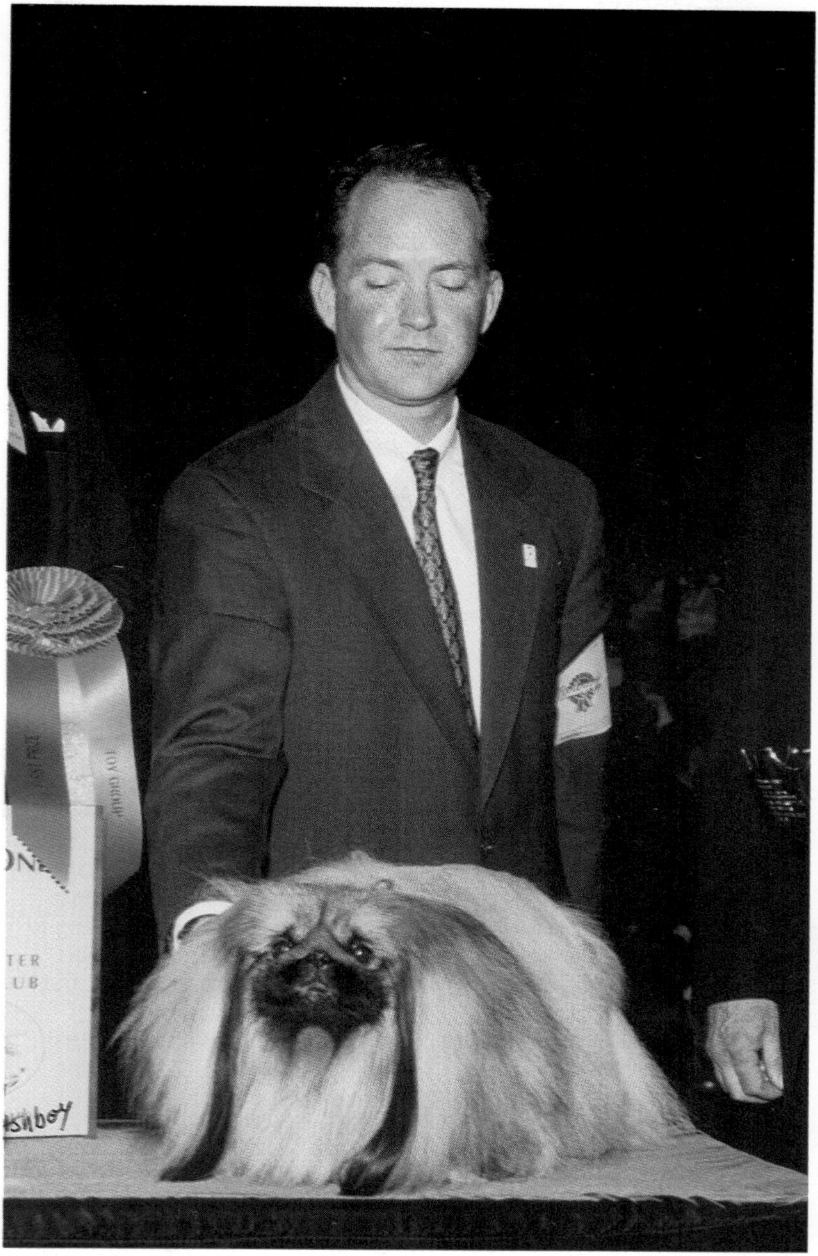

*Ch. Briarcourt's Damien Gable winning Group 1 placement at the Westminster Kennel Club Dog Show, 1994. Owner, Nancy H. Shapland.*

Some breeds, particularly hunting dogs and some of the hounds, also compete in field trials.

There are three classes in obedience: Novice, Open, and Utility. Tracking tests also are held. The respective degrees earned are: C.D., C.D.X., U.D., and T.D. These are: Companion Dog, Companion Dog Excellent, Utility Dog, and Tracking Dog. To earn a C.D., both the dog and his handler must perform six exercises together to the satisfaction of three different judges. Judges score the teams on a scale of zero to 200 points, and a score of 170 points or higher earns a dog a "leg" toward his obedience degree. A dog must achieve three "legs" for a C.D. Exercises in this Novice Class are: heel on lead and figure eight, stand for examination by a judge, heel off lead, long sit (sitting for a required number of minutes), long down (being down for several minutes), and recall (returning to his owner when called). After a dog gets his C.D., he then may try for his C.D.X. in Open obedience where he must jump over obstacles, retrieve items, and do more difficult exercises in three different trials. To achieve a U.D. title, a dog must do directed retrieving, jumping, and scent discrimination. To obtain a tracking degree, a dog competes in field trials where he "tracks" or follows a scent.

## PRE-SHOW PREPARATIONS

As a very basic guide, the following list has been compiled to help you with your preparations for your first point show: the identification ticket sent by the show superintendent, a grooming table, a sturdy tack box in which to carry your dog's grooming tools, a leash to fasten him to the bench or stall and another show lead, your first aid kit, packaged "dog treats," and a supply of food and water for man and beast. Take the largest thermos you can find and a water dish. Remember to feed your dog after the show, not before, and make certain that he exercises and relieves himself before he enters the ring. Many experts think that an exercise pen is mandatory to eliminate the risk of exposing your dog to any diseases in the common exercise ground at shows, but before you bring one along, check the show rules to see if these are allowed. Moreover, exercise pens are useful as places where your dog can stretch out or rest during your travels or at a motel.

Even take time to think about what you are going to wear on the big day; sports clothes and

# AMERICAN DOG SHOW JUDGING PROCEDURE

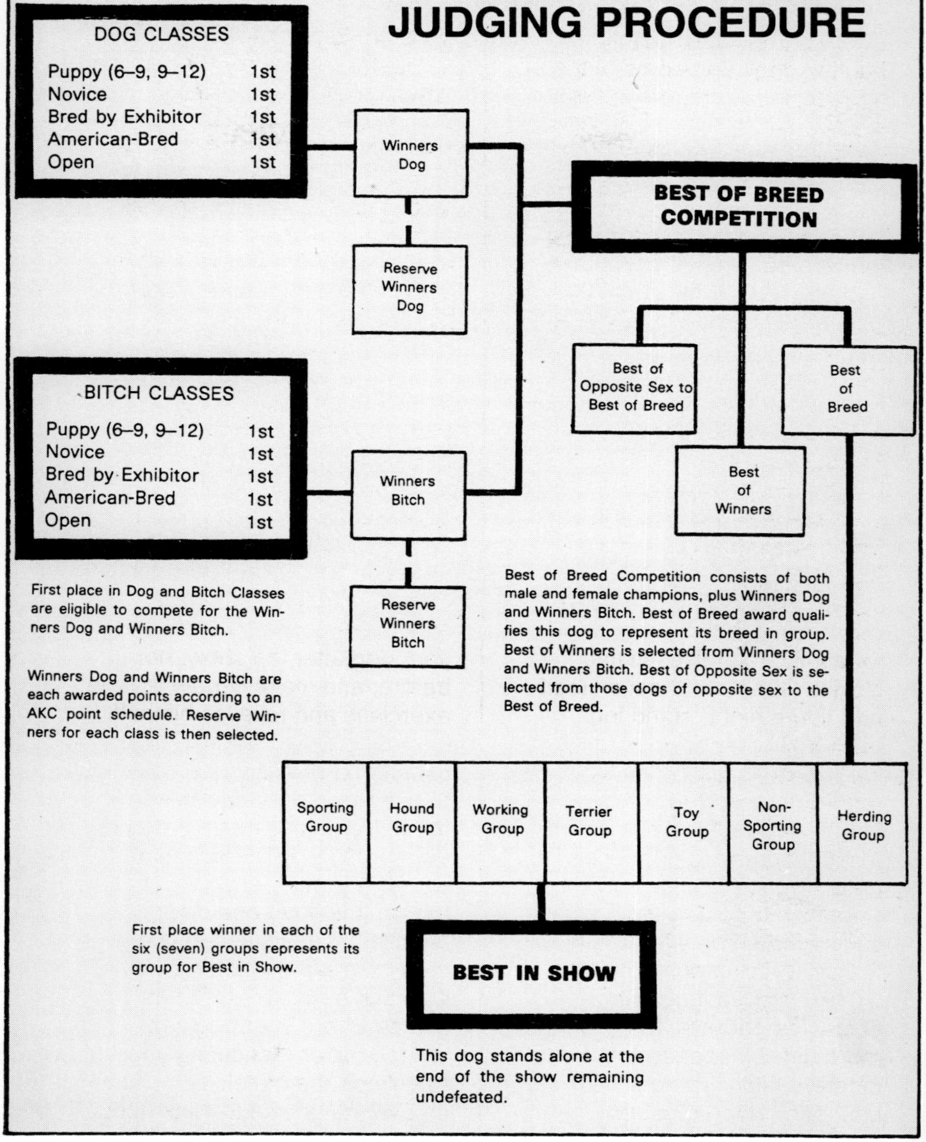

***The expression of the Pekingese should suggest the breed's Chinese origin in its quaintness and individuality.***

low-heeled, comfortable shoes are the best. You certainly do not want to wear anything that would distract the judge's attention from your dog; you should merely provide an attractive background for him.

Although your knees may be trembling, try to appear self-confident as you gait (move) and set up the dog. The judging routine usually begins when the judge asks that the dogs be gaited in a circle around the ring while he observes their style, topline, head and tail carriage, reach and drive, and general balance. Avoid going too close to the dog in front of you. Make certain that the judge has an unrestricted view of your dog by keeping him on the inside of the circle, between you and the judge.

**DOG SHOW ETIQUETTE**

There are a few "golden rules" to be followed at dog shows which are worth mentioning at this stage. First of all, you are responsible for the behavior of your dog at all times. Keep your dog with you until the showing and keep him under control at all times. Constant vigilance is necessary as thefts have been known at dog shows, as well as poisoning and physical abuse of the animals by jealous exhibitors. You do not want your dog to become involved in a dog fight or taken for a walk by an irresponsible child or one too young to discipline him. In other words, you must not let your dog out of your sight.

Another golden rule is to be punctual; do not be late for your class. Remember that in the ring

*Dog show exhibitors must be prepared to supervise and clean up after their dogs whenever on show grounds.*

*Squeaky toys and fuzzy animals are excellent tools to bait a dog in the show ring. Be sure not to distract your dog when the judge is examining him.*

you must not communicate with the judge or fellow competitors. Watch the judge carefully and follow his instructions. Bear in mind that the ring is not the place to discipline or train your dog; it is too late at this stage! Whatever the judge's decision, accept it with good grace whether you win or lose. *Never* argue with a judge. Finally, remember to praise your dog for his efforts. It has been a long day for him as well.

**"DOUBLE HANDLING"**

Only one person should be handling your dog; there should not be other "handlers" in the audience who hope to influence his performance by the well-timed whistle, the "spontaneous" applause, or the secret signal. Such tactics are unsportsmanlike as they often distract the attention of other dogs. This so-called "double handling" is frowned upon by the American Kennel Club as a desperate measure resorted to by a desperate owner. Moreover, to try to prompt a win or stir up interest in your dog by bringing along your own cheering section is a futile gesture as a judge is concentrating on what he is doing and is not influenced by such subversive strategy. These people seem to be declaring that their dog cannot win by its own merits under normal conditions but needs some extra assistance.

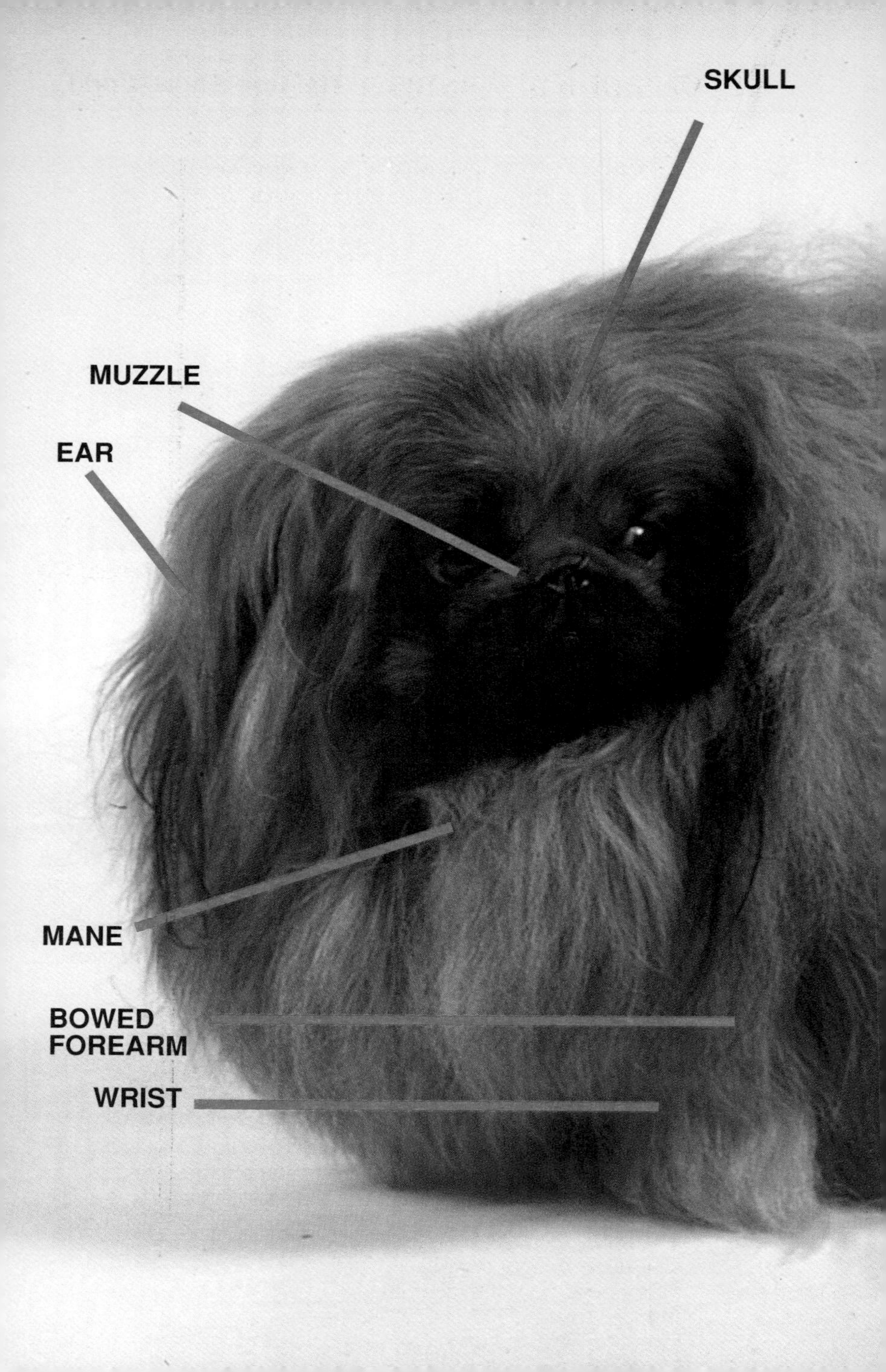
SKULL
MUZZLE
EAR
MANE
BOWED
FOREARM
WRIST

# Topographical Anatomy of the Pekingese

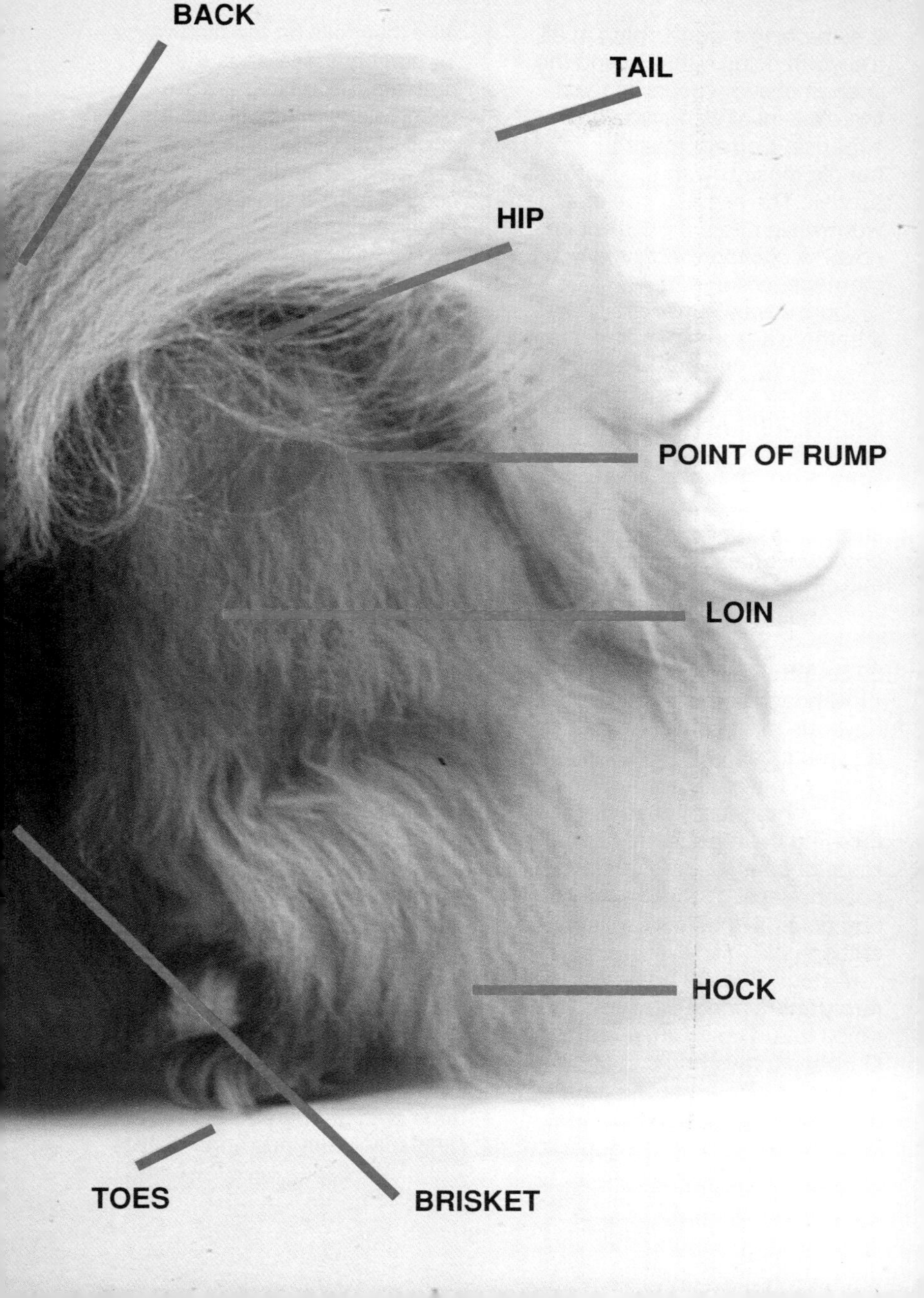

# Owner Concerns

By Chris Walkowicz

If something's worth doing at all, it's worth doing right. Behind the scenes of every gourmet feast, there's a lot of work, time and expense. Someone has to handle messy clean-up chores as well. The same is true of any worthwhile effort: a prize-winning novel, a community play, a good marriage, children, pets.

Conscientious owners know that there's more to raising a dog than picking one out, feeding it once a day and petting it if they feel the urge. Just as a fancy restaurant includes fine linens, flowers on the table and an attractive ambiance with the sustenance, being a top-quality dog owner means more than tossing a bone in the backyard now and then.

## STRAYS

Although some people still have the mistaken idea that "a dog must be free," most are discovering that the world isn't what it once was. Loose dogs enjoying their "freedom" face all kinds of traumas: shotguns, poison, traps, oncoming trucks, dog pounds and the resulting euthanasia.

A dog without a home can rarely find a handout or even a rabbit to run down anymore. Garbage forays don't go far enough to fill an empty stomach, and they anger the person who is left to pick up the mess. Cars take their tolls on the highways. To combat these and other problems, good owners are taking steps to make sure their dogs remain welcome in society.

When a breeder is first contacted by a prospective buyer, the question is not simply, "Do you have a fenced yard?" but "Do you have a pen or a fenced yard—or do you plan to walk your dog on leash?" No option. If "none of the above" is the answer, it's bye-bye, buyer.

Children who are uncontrolled and unrestricted are obnoxious, cause damage and are a danger to themselves. Responsible people know that when they tell their children "No," it really is for their own good and that of others. It's not just a power ploy to deny them a privilege. Although it is difficult, there are reasons parents deny complete freedom to children, and there are reasons to deny it to dogs.

Dogs will be dogs. Loose animals are, at the least, a pain in the posterior and, at worst, a threat to themselves and others. Stray dogs bite, poop, scare kids, chase people, strew garbage, ruin lawns and gardens, kill other animals and produce unwanted litters.

## OVERPOPULATION

The number of once-upon-a-time pets humanely euthanized annually in pounds and shelters is mind-boggling. These and the additional number of animals who die in agony—starvation, abuse, disease, trauma or road kills—were murdered by irresponsible owners and breeders as surely as if they aimed a gun and pulled the trigger. If animals were considered as living creatures instead of property by the court systems, many owners could be charged with negligence in their pets' deaths.

Neutering (spaying and castrating) means fewer animals, and fewer animals enable us to decrease the horrible statistics. Not only do we ascertain that none of our dog's pups become part of the canine carnage, but neutering also lowers the percentage of cancers and diseases of the reproductive system.

There are already plenty of dogs in the world without creating more. Anyone who wants one can find one immediately. It's only when people want specifics (i.e., a Pointer with great hunting ability; a Saint Bernard with lines that are hip-certified and show longevity; a Dachshund pup with the potential to go Best in Show) that someone needs to supply a demand.

It is true that a mixed-breed dog can make a great pet. Any dog, even one whose background is unknown, might turn into your best pal. But you're taking your chances. There are already thousands of those to go around—no need to create more. Only someone who cares enough to obtain the knowledge to produce canines with specific physical characteristics, temperament and instincts has a right to add to the already-bulging and suffering canine population. Therefore, ethical breeders now sell companion pups with a spay/neuter clause, which requires the dog to be neutered at puberty or by the age of one year. Many also use the Limited Registration option with the American Kennel Club. This allows the dog itself to be registered and shown in obedience and instinct tests, but in case of a "mistake," none of its progeny can be registered.

Dog breeding, done properly, is an expensive proposition. It is also time-consuming, extra work, occasionally heartbreaking and often frustrating. Add all of these problems to the fact that a neutered pet is a healthier one, many pet—and even some show—owners now choose a sexless life for their dog.

## LICENSING

Dog licenses are not another means to extract more money from your pocket for the local government, but rather they are

The flowing mane of the Pekingese has made him known as the "Lion Dog." Owner, Diane Renchan.

insurance for your dog. A dog license just might save your pet from euthanasia. Animal control officers compare the dog license to our own driver's licenses. It's an I.D. That tag hanging from his collar can be traced to the owner, which means a lost pet might be saved from the gas chamber. Licenses also contribute toward the care of the unwanted, forgotten and forlorn ex-pets who will pay the price for "freedom."

## THEFT AND LOSS

It's terrifying when a dog owner first looks outdoors and sees the empty yard with the gate swinging open. When someone realizes his pet is gone, the heart takes a plummeting ride to the pit of the stomach.

Sometimes, no matter what precautions are taken, accidents happen—a child leaves a gate open or a well-behaved dog finds a rabbit on the other side of the fence too attractive to resist.

Owners should take action immediately to assure the pet's return. Don't wait a few hours to see if he'll come home. It may be too late.

**To find a lost dog:**

**1. Posters**—Have hundreds printed at a jiffy printer, preferably with a photo, and post every one. Someone who sees one poster may not retain the memory, but someone who sees 20 will remember. Describe the dog, always keeping in mind the fable of the blind men and the elephant. To a large man, a medium-sized dog may appear to be small; to a child, it may seem to be an elephant. In addition, a lost dog usually loses weight. It's better to print a lower estimate of his size and describe the breed, even if it's a well-known breed. Remember if the dog is gone for more than a few hours, a well-groomed animal can quickly become disheveled and appear unkempt.

**2. Spread the word**—Tell the mail carrier (who's always on the alert for stray dogs). Call the neighbors and schools (kids enjoy helping and love dogs). Call the police, veterinarians, pounds, shelters and humane societies not only in your county but in the surrounding counties. Dogs travel many miles in search of the cat they spied . . . or home. Not all dogs have the homing instinct of Lassie. As soon as possible, visit animal organizations with your posters. Don't take their word that there is no such purebred on the premises. Most people wouldn't recognize one if it bit them—and then it would probably be too late.

**3. Advertise**—Call the papers and the radio stations. Offer a reward (which should also be printed on the posters). Make it high enough to make it worthwhile for someone to return the dog, but low enough that it does not invite extortionists.

**4. Search**—Never stop searching. Use an answering machine or have someone stay by the phone to answer any reports of the dog being sighted. Dogs have been found as long as six months after their loss.

**5. Humane trap**—Set a familiar object (a blanket or a crate with a favorite toy) on your porch or in your garage, along with bowls of food and water. If he does come home while you're out searching, he'll have a reason to stay.

**6. Prevention**—Fences, kennel runs and walking on leash. If the dog is a jumper or climber, make the fence higher or plant shrubs around to increase the distance and top the run. I.D. your dog with tags and a tattoo. Take photos, both *haute coiffure* and *au naturel.*

**7. Be prepared**—A lost dog is often terrified. Even those who are normally friendly can panic when called by a stranger, or even by someone they've known and loved all their lives. Use a lure: food, a kennelmate, an open car door, a bitch in season for a stud dog, a favorite toy or sound (like food pans, or a gunshot for a hunting dog).

Too often, also, dognappers are lured by a winsome face, easy prey, or the potential easy money flashed by a purebred. The dognapper's booty is sometimes sold to people who are unaware of the circumstances. Sometimes, however, they're sold to people who fake papers and resell the dog. Worse yet, they might be sold to dog fighters (as bait or fighters) or laboratories (for experiments). Stolen dogs are difficult, if not impossible, to trace unless they can be positively identified.

### TATTOO IDENTIFICATION

To prevent a much-loved family pet from ending his days in fear and agony, the best method of prevention is tattooing. Many dog clubs and veterinarians provide tattoo identification. By law, no laboratory may use a dog bearing a tattoo. Although some owners tattoo on the inside of the ear, most choose the inside of the rear thigh. An ear can be easily cut off.

Most American owners use their social security number, which is usually put on the inside of the dog's right hind thigh. Some use the dog's registration number, which goes on the inside of the left rear thigh. The area is first shaved and numbed. There is no pain, although a few dogs do not like the buzzing sound.

*The Pekingese body should be short, heavy in front with a broad chest. The coat is long and straight, with the profuse mane extending beyond the shoulders and forming a cape around the neck. Owner, Diane Renchan.*

**NO DOGS!**

In Europe, dogs accompany their masters everywhere—to stores, buses and even in restaurants. Because the dogs are accustomed to public acceptance, they're well behaved and sit or lie quietly. Or is it because the pets are well behaved that they are accepted?

In the United States, however, "No Dogs"! signs are popping up like weeds—all over and too many. Because of bratty canines and careless owners, landlords demand a no-pets clause in leases. Parks restrict certain areas for pets if they're allowed at all. Many motels and hotels no longer admit anyone with a dog.

Many cities have a poop-scoop ordinance. Owners are required to clean up after their dogs or pay a fine. For too long, people have had the mistaken notion that their bad habits are not offensive to others, or even if they are, that's tough luck. These people claim, "It's our right to leave doggy doo-doo (drive carelessly, be sloppy drunk, blow smoke in your face or you fill in the blank). We aren't hurting anyone." Wrong. It's our right to own dogs but not to turn parks, sidewalks and public places into doggy latrines. Now we know our bad habits can be not only offensive but harmful to others, and we've got to straighten up and fly right, or we'll be flying solo.

If we want to continue this special bond between dogs and people, we must scoop poop, walk dogs on leash and train them to behave in public. It's no longer a good idea but a necessity that we attend classes and practice good manners. That demands confining pets and curtailing barking. It means no destruction of motel rooms, no jumping up when uninvited and no disgusting piles left behind—in other words, cleaning up our act.

**RESCUE**

Dog fanciers have recognized the need to spread good will beyond the home boundaries. There are too many strays, abuse cases and abandoned animals. Dogs in these situations need help, and they can't supply it themselves. Their so-called owners won't supply it.

Local and national clubs have organized rescue associations to aid in placing these needy dogs. Members volunteer to investigate situations, check out shelters and even to house a victim temporarily. Because of conditions where the animals may have suffered physically as well as mentally, many dogs need TLC and veterinary treatment before a new home is sought. Usually the dog is neutered before placement.

Occasionally, there is a waiting list for "orphans of the storm." Other times, a dog must be maintained and made well again before being adopted. All prospective homes are thoroughly screened so that the tragedy does not reoccur.

Medical care, boarding, adoption fees, transportation and routine expenses all mean that breed rescue programs need funds. Some samaritans foot the bills themselves. Clubs hold fundraising occasions which include bake sales, garage sales, recycling, tattoo clinics, auctions, matches, dog washes and dips and a rescue "check-off" included with the check for annual dues. Recipients of rescued dogs often respond and are, in some cases, required to make donations.

When these dogs are once again sound, they are placed in good homes. In this way, club members feel they are giving something back to the breed they love so much.

Breeders can assist in assuring that their pups won't someday be in need of rescue by including return clauses in their contracts. The breeder should always have first option to take the dog back if he needs to be placed. Follow up on pups with inquiries to see how they're doing, requests for photos to fill the breeder's scrapbook, and suggestions of training classes. Offering your assistance to groom or handle the dog and your availability to answer questions will help the new owner make it through tough times and offer assurance that one of your pups won't become a victim of our throw-away society.

### PETS AND HEALTH: A FRIEND INDEED

*By Diana Schellenberg*

*Excerpted from the December 1993 issue of the HARVARD HEALTH LETTER, ©1993, President and Fellows of Harvard College.*

"I think I could turn and live with animals," Walt Whitman wrote, "they are so placid and self-contained." And as T. S. Eliot pointed out, animals are "such agreeable friends—they ask no questions, they pass no criticisms." Apparently the majority of Americans agree with the poets: 58% of households in the United States now include at least one pet. A 1992 survey sponsored by the American Veterinary Medical Association showed that cats, with a population of around 60 million, have surpassed dogs as America's favorite companion animal—a shift that probably comes as no surprise to cats, who have always acted as though they were number one. What with the cats and around

*The Pekingese muzzle should be wrinkled, very short and broad, not overshot nor pointed. Owner, Diane Renchan.*

52 million dogs, 12 million birds, and 5 million horses, Americans are sharing their daily lives with nearly 130 million of these creatures. In addition, around 8% of households keep fish and at least 4% have more unusual pets such as ferrets, gerbils, rabbits, or reptiles.

Most people who have companion animals consider them members of the family. Unlike humans in the household who have their ups and downs, most pets behave in fairly predictable ways and many offer unconditional affection. Dogs and cats typically spend most of their time in the house, and many sleep on their owners' beds. One measure of the value of their company is the billions of dollars that Americans spend each year on pet food, accessories, and veterinary care. And everyone has read about the elaborate markers that grieving pet owners erect to memorialize their departed companions.

**Baby talk**

People enjoy their animals, and being with them stirs a sense of security and of being needed. Pets, regardless of their age, fill the role of an infant or young child in the household, according to researcher Alan Beck, who heads the Center for Applied Ethology and Human-Animal Interaction at the Purdue University School of Veterinary Medicine. He and psychiatrist Aaron Katcher did pioneering studies of the connection between humans and animals during the 1970s and 1980s, when both were at the University of Pennsylvania.

Drs. Beck and Katcher found that people talk to their pets as if they were young infants. They move close to the animal's head, use a higher-pitched voice, and speak more softly and slowly than usual. They insert pauses as if the animal were answering back. Their facial expressions also soften, which may be one reason why people are perceived as more attractive and more approachable when they are with a pet.

**Warm fuzzies**

Only during the past few decades have scientists become interested in the beneficial effects that pets may have on human health. One way to assess the effect is to measure the short-term physiological impact of contact with an animal. So far, experiments using children and college students have found that watching or petting and talking with an animal can lower blood pressure and heart rate.

Short-term studies have also demonstrated that interacting with animals can reduce mental distress. For college students in a laboratory setting, petting a friendly dog lowered not only their blood pressure and heart rate but also their anxiety level, as measured by a standard test. Researchers found that patients who watched fish in an aquarium while they waited to have oral surgery did just as well as those who underwent hypnosis to reduce anxiety and discomfort during the surgery. These results help explain why aquariums are so popular in dental and medical waiting rooms.

Most epidemiologic studies comparing people with and without pets have suggested that those who share their lives with animals have higher morale and lower rates of depression. Such studies do not tell us, however, whether pet owning leads to better psychological health or whether it's healthier people who acquire pets in the first place.

**Heartfelt support**

A large Australian study reported in 1992 did not answer this question but did indicate that pet owners have fewer risk factors for heart disease than people without such companions. The researchers assessed common predictors of cardiovascular problems in 5,741 people who attended a free screening clinic in Melbourne. Overall, the 13.6% who owned pets had lower systolic blood pressure and lower total cholesterol and triglyceride levels than non-owners. These differences were significant despite variations in participants' smoking habits, diet, body height and weight, and socioeconomic status. It did not appear to matter if pets had four legs, wings, or scales: all pet owners benefited whether or not they had pets that needed regular exercise.

Although the association between pet ownership and an apparent reduction in cardiovascular risk is an interesting finding, it does not demonstrate that pets can guard their masters against heart disease or any other illness. This kind of evidence can be gained only from *prospective* studies, where researchers, in anticipation of possible patterns or correlations, design research to analyze ongoing events. In this instance, researchers would need to track the health status of many pet owners and non-owners over a long period of time.

So far, the largest prospective investigation of the effect of pet owning was done by epidemiologist Judith Siegel of the University of California, Los Angeles. For one year Dr. Siegel monitored stressful life

The large, dark, round, and lustrous eyes of the Pekingese quaintly portray his sincere loyalty and devotion.

events, use of physician services, and the psychological well-being of 938 people who were covered by Medicare and enrolled in a health maintenance organization. The 37% of participants who owned pets made fewer visits to the doctor than people without animal companions. This was true regardless of the chronic health problems they had at the beginning of the study period, or of their sex, age, race, education, income, employment status, and degree of social support from other people.

When family members or friends became severely ill or died, pets seemed to be a "stress buffer" for their bereaved human companions. People without pets made more physician visits as stressful events accumulated in their lives, but pet owners—especially those with dogs—did not follow this pattern. Reporting her findings in the *Journal of Personality and Social Psychology,* Dr. Siegel speculated that elderly people sometimes go to the doctor because they need companionship, or because loneliness exacerbates their health concerns.

Pets, particularly dogs, appear at least partially to satisfy the need for company. About 25% of people in Dr. Siegel's study said that their pets made them feel secure, and 21% said they felt loved by their animals. These findings, coupled with results from smaller inquiries, suggest that the social and psychological support that people gain from pets may reduce their need for the attention of health care providers.

Animal companionship may also be a boon to people recovering from an acute illness. A prospective study of 92 people admitted to a coronary care unit for confirmed or suspected myocardial infarction found that those with animals were more likely to be alive one year later than those without pets.

**The dark underbelly**

The benefits of pet owning seem so obvious—especially after a brisk walk with a lively dog or an evening curled up with a purring puss—that it is tempting to brush aside the negative aspects of living with animals. Unfortunately, problems can arise from allergies, bites, or infections.

Roughly 1.5% of the general population and 25% of patients being treated for allergies are sensitive to dogs or cats. When doctors recommend that the offending animal be removed from the home, pet-owning patients often resist. Recent research suggests that people who are allergic to cats may be able to coexist with them if they wash the cat once a week, accustom the animal to spending more time outdoors, eliminate carpeting, use air filters, and follow a rigorous housecleaning schedule. (Researchers, however, do not report what sort of protective gear pet owners should don for the weekly bath.)

Animal bites pose an even more obvious health problem. Bites account for 1% of all visits to hospital emergency rooms, although about 80% of these injuries are minor. Many bites need not have occurred in the first place. Children should be taught how to approach and handle pets, read their warning signals, and avoid high-risk situations. Dog owners must do their part by training their dogs and by keeping potentially dangerous animals leashed or fenced.

Infectious diseases can be spread when a bite deposits organisms from the animal's mouth into a wound. These infections range from the annoying to the potentially deadly, such as rabies. Any bite that breaks the skin calls for prompt medical attention. Fortunately, taking a few simple measures can reduce the risk.

The difficulty of balancing the benefits and risks of sharing one's life with an animal may be illustrated most poignantly by the pet owner with AIDS, who needs a loving companion but whose impaired immune system is particularly vulnerable to certain infections. Volunteer organizations help AIDS patients keep their pets by offering food deliveries, in-home pet care, foster care, and adoption services when the need arises.

**Prescription pets**

In the therapeutic arena, there is a growing appreciation for the roles that companion animals can play in institutions and in the world at large. Dogs have long been used as a source of support for troubled children and for psychiatric patients, and today many volunteers take their pets to visit local nursing homes. Assistance dogs serve as surrogate eyes, ears, or legs for thousands of people with disabilities.

For most people pets are neither a panacea nor a plague. Responsible pet ownership entails a commitment to the animal and a promise to train it properly and to provide it with adequate care. The return on this investment can be considerable: a loving companion, an antidote to stress, and perhaps a reason for regular exercise, all wrapped up in fur or feathers.

# Breeding

As the owner of a purebred dog, you may have considered breeding your pet at one time or another. If your dog is a beloved family pet, and not a show dog, you should *not* breed your dog. Breeding is not a hobby for pet owners, but rather a demanding, complicated vocation that is not to be dabbled with. Many people have thought of breeding as an easy-money opportunity: buy two dogs and let them do the work. The rule of thumb is: if you're making money by breeding dogs, you're doing something wrong!

Consider the time and money involved just to get your bitch into breeding condition and then to sustain her throughout pregnancy and afterwards while she tends her young. You will be obligated to house, feed, groom, and housebreak the puppies until good homes can be found for them; and, lest we forget, there will be periodic trips to the vet for check-ups, wormings, and inoculations. Common sense should tell you that it is indeed cruel to bring unwanted or unplanned puppies into an already crowded canine world; only negligent pet owners allow this to happen. Recognizing the number of dogs, purebred and mixed breeds, pet-, show- and breeding-quality, that are put to sleep annually, responsible breeders require that all pet animals be neutered. This condition most often is incorporated into the selling contract. The motives of good breeders are clear: avoid the manufacturing and mass-producing of average and below-average dogs; control the overblown canine population; concentrate on the improvement of purebred bloodlines. Breeding is a noble calling and unless you can improve the breed, you should not consider breeding your animal. Despite all of the obvious virtues of breeding texts, no book could ever prepare a person for breeding. What a heart-breaking and tragic experience to lose an entire litter because a good-intentioned pet owner wasn't aware of potential genetic complications, didn't recognize a breech birth, or couldn't identify the signals of a struggling bitch! Possibly the dam could be lost as well!

Before you take any step towards mating your bitch, think carefully about why you want her to give birth to a litter of puppies. If you feel she will be deprived in some way if she is not bred, if you think your children will learn from the experience, if you have the mistaken notion that you will make money from this great undertaking, think again. A dog can lead a perfectly happy, healthy, normal life without having been mated; in fact, spaying a female and neuterin a male helps them become better, longer-lived pets, as they are not so anxious to search for a mate in an effort to relieve their sexual tensions and have a diminished risk of cancer. As for giving the children a lesson in sex education, this is hardly a valid reason for breeding your dog. And on an economic level, it takes not only years of hard work (researching pedigrees and bloodlines, studying genetics, among other things), but it takes plenty of capital (money, equipment, facilities) to make a decent profit from dog breeding. Why most dedicated breeders are lucky just to break even. If you have only a casual interest in dog breeding, it is best to leave this pastime to those who are more experienced in such matters, those who consider it a serious hobby and a real vocation. If you have bought a breeder– or show-quality canine, one that may be capable of producing champions, and if you are just starting out with this

*Breeding dogs requires more than book knowledge. In dogs, breech presentation is not uncommon and the breeder must be prepared to handle this situation and guide the puppy so that neither the pup nor the bitch is injured.*

breeding venture, seek advice from the seller of your dog, from other veteran breeders, and from your veterinarian before you begin.

The following sections on reproduction are intended for academic value only. This is not a "How-to" chapter on breeding, nor a step-by-step approach for the novice for getting started. Hopefully the reader will understand the depth and complexity of breeding as well as the expected ethical and moral obligations of persons who choose to do so—and never attempt it.

## THE FEMALE "IN SEASON"

A bitch may come into season (also known as "heat" or estrus) once or several times a year, depending on the particular breed and the individual dog. Her first seasonal period, that is to say, the time when she is capable of being fertilized by a male dog, may occur as early as six months with some breeds. If you own a female and your intention is *not* to breed her, by

*Ideally the puppy will be delivered in the normal head-first position.*

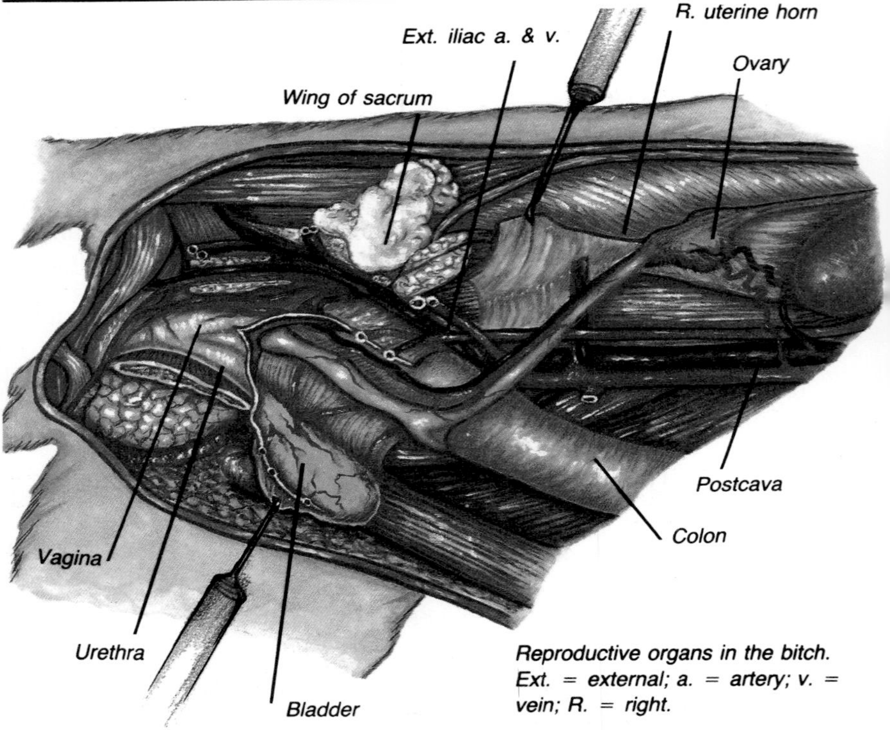


*Reproductive organs in the bitch. Ext. = external; a. = artery; v. = vein; R. = right.*

*The reproductive system of the female dog consists of a highly specialized system of organs situated to the rear of the animal.*

all means discuss with the vet the possibility of having her spayed: this means before she reaches sexual maturity.

The first sign of the female's being in season is a thin red discharge, which may increase for about a week; it then changes color to a thin yellowish stain, which lasts about another week. Simultaneously, there is a swelling of the vulva, the exterior portion of the female's reproductive tract; the soft, flabby vulva indicates her readiness to mate. Around this second week or so ovulation occurs, and this is the crucial period for her to be bred, if this is what you have in mind for her. It is during this middle phase of the heat cycle when conception can take place. Just remember that there is great variation from bitch to bitch with regard to how often they come into heat, how long the heat cycles last, how long the period of ovulation lasts, and how much time elapses between heat cycles. Generally, after the third week of heat, the vulval swelling decreases and the estrus period ceases for several months.

It should be mentioned that the female will probably lose her puppy coat, or at least shed part of it, about three months after she has come into season. This is the time when her puppies would have been weaned, had she been mated, and females generally drop coat at this time.

With female dogs, there are few, if any, behavioral changes during estrus. A bitch may dart out of an open door to greet all available male dogs that show an interest in her, and she may occasionally raise her tail and

*Each egg within the female is surrounded by a wall that normally takes many sperm to penetrate. In this way, it is more likely that only the strongest sperm will fertilize the egg. A fertile female in season usually has a number of eggs, known as gametes.*

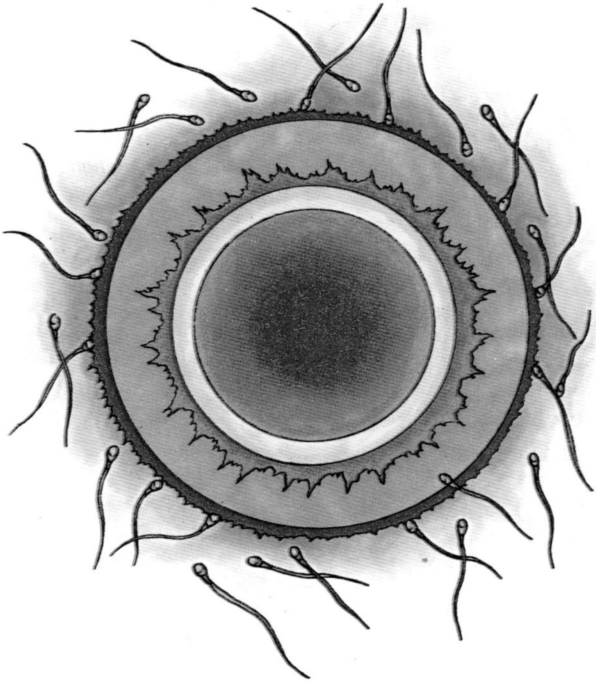

assume a mating stance, particularly if you pet her lower back; but these signs are not as dramatic as those of the sexually mature male. He himself does not experience heat cycles; rather, he is attracted to the female during all phases of her seasonal period. He usually becomes more aggressive and tends to fight with other males, especially over females in heat. He tends to mark his territory with urine to attract females and at the same time to warn other competitive males. It is not uncommon to see him mount various objects, and people, in an effort to satisfy his mature sexual urges.

If you are a homeowner and you have an absolutely climb-proof and dig-proof run within your yard, it may be safe to leave your bitch in season there. But then again it may not be a wise idea, as there have been cases of males mating with females right through chain-link fencing! Just to be on the safe side, shut her indoors during her heat periods and don't let her outdoors until you are certain the estrus period is over. Never leave a bitch in heat outdoors, unsupervised, even for a minute so that she can defecate or urinate. If you want to prevent the neighborhood dogs from hanging around your doorstep, as they inevitably will do when they discover your female is in season, take her some distance away from the house before you let her do her business. Otherwise, these canine suitors will be attracted to her by the arousing odor of her urine, and they will know instinctively that she isn't far from her scented "calling card." If you need to walk your bitch, take her in the car to a nearby park or field for a chance to stretch her legs. Remember that after about three weeks, and this varies from dog to dog, you can let her outdoors again with no worry that she can have puppies until the next heat period.

If you are seriously considering breeding your dog, first talk to as many experienced breeders as possible and read up on the subject in specific books and articles. Only when you are fully aware of the demands and responsibilities of breeding should you make your final decision. It must be stated here that there is no shortage of fine dogs in need of good homes, nor is there likely to be in the foreseeable future. So, if

***Facing page:*** *The male reproductive system includes the penis and testicles. When not excited, the penis is withdrawn into the dog's body.*

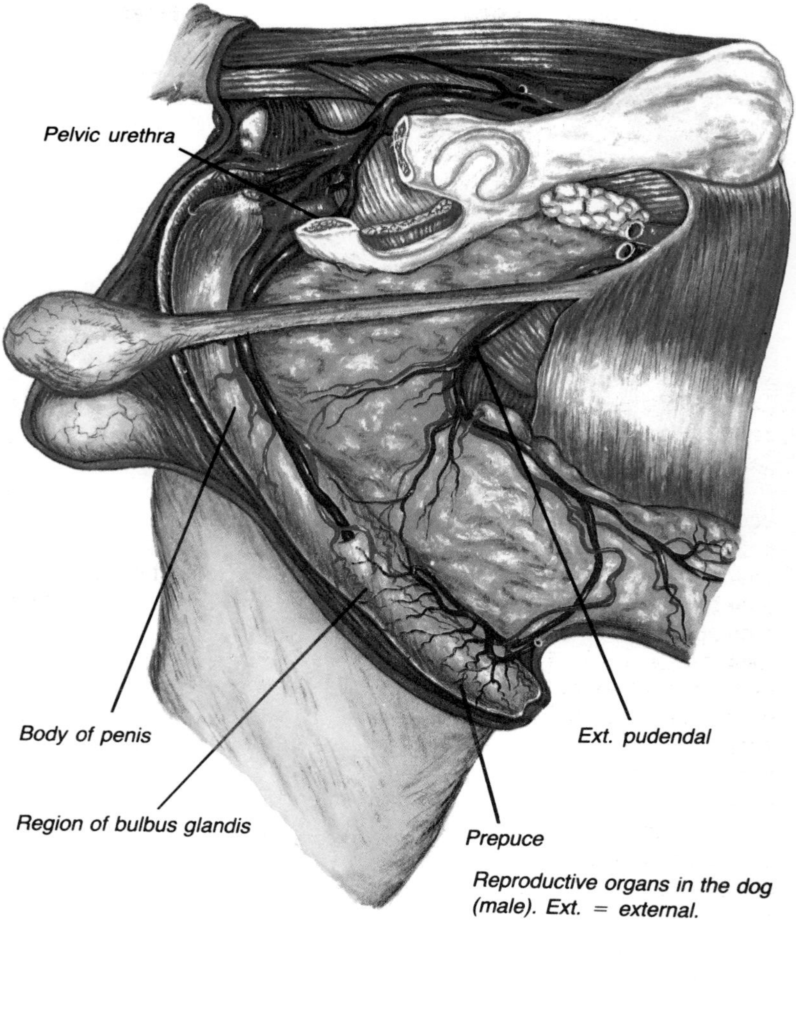


Reproductive organs in the dog (male). Ext. = external.

# PERPETUAL WHELPING CHART

| | | | |
|---|---|---|---|
| Bred—Jan. | 1 2 3 4 5 6 7 8 9 10 11 12 13 14 15 16 17 18 19 20 21 22 23 24 25 26 27 | | 28 29 30 31 |
| Due—March | 5 6 7 8 9 10 11 12 13 14 15 16 17 18 19 20 21 22 23 24 25 26 27 28 29 30 31 | April | 1 2 3 4 |
| Bred—Feb. | 1 2 3 4 5 6 7 8 9 10 11 12 13 14 15 16 17 18 19 20 21 22 23 24 25 26 | | 27 28 |
| Due—April | 5 6 7 8 9 10 11 12 13 14 15 16 17 18 19 20 21 22 23 24 25 26 27 28 29 30 | May | 1 2 |
| Bred—Mar. | 1 2 3 4 5 6 7 8 9 10 11 12 13 14 15 16 17 18 19 20 21 22 23 24 25 26 27 28 29 | | 30 31 |
| Due—May | 3 4 5 6 7 8 9 10 11 12 13 14 15 16 17 18 19 20 21 22 23 24 25 26 27 28 29 30 31 | June | 1 2 |
| Bred—Apr. | 1 2 3 4 5 6 7 8 9 10 11 12 13 14 15 16 17 18 19 20 21 22 23 24 25 26 27 28 | | 29 30 |
| Due—June | 3 4 5 6 7 8 9 10 11 12 13 14 15 16 17 18 19 20 21 22 23 24 25 26 27 28 29 30 | July | 1 2 |
| Bred—May | 1 2 3 4 5 6 7 8 9 10 11 12 13 14 15 16 17 18 19 20 21 22 23 24 25 26 27 28 29 | | 30 31 |
| Due—July | 3 4 5 6 7 8 9 10 11 12 13 14 15 16 17 18 19 20 21 22 23 24 25 26 27 28 29 30 31 | August | 1 2 |
| Bred—June | 1 2 3 4 5 6 7 8 9 10 11 12 13 14 15 16 17 18 19 20 21 22 23 24 25 26 27 28 29 | | 30 |
| Due—August | 3 4 5 6 7 8 9 10 11 12 13 14 15 16 17 18 19 20 21 22 23 24 25 26 27 28 29 30 31 | Sept. | 1 |
| Bred—July | 1 2 3 4 5 6 7 8 9 10 11 12 13 14 15 16 17 18 19 20 21 22 23 24 25 26 27 28 29 | | 30 31 |
| Due—September | 2 3 4 5 6 7 8 9 10 11 12 13 14 15 16 17 18 19 20 21 22 23 24 25 26 27 28 29 30 | Oct. | 1 2 |
| Bred—Aug. | 1 2 3 4 5 6 7 8 9 10 11 12 13 14 15 16 17 18 19 20 21 22 23 24 25 26 27 28 29 | | 30 31 |
| Due—October | 3 4 5 6 7 8 9 10 11 12 13 14 15 16 17 18 19 20 21 22 23 24 25 26 27 28 29 30 31 | Nov. | 1 2 |
| Bred—Sept. | 1 2 3 4 5 6 7 8 9 10 11 12 13 14 15 16 17 18 19 20 21 22 23 24 25 26 27 28 | | 29 30 |
| Due—November | 3 4 5 6 7 8 9 10 11 12 13 14 15 16 17 18 19 20 21 22 23 24 25 26 27 28 29 30 | Dec. | 1 2 |
| Bred—Oct. | 1 2 3 4 5 6 7 8 9 10 11 12 13 14 15 16 17 18 19 20 21 22 23 24 25 26 27 28 29 | | 30 31 |
| Due—December | 3 4 5 6 7 8 9 10 11 12 13 14 15 16 17 18 19 20 21 22 23 24 25 26 27 28 29 30 31 | Jan. | 1 2 |
| Bred—Nov. | 1 2 3 4 5 6 7 8 9 10 11 12 13 14 15 16 17 18 19 20 21 22 23 24 25 26 27 28 29 | | 30 |
| Due—January | 3 4 5 6 7 8 9 10 11 12 13 14 15 16 17 18 19 20 21 22 23 24 25 26 27 28 29 30 31 | Feb. | 1 |
| Bred—Dec. | 1 2 3 4 5 6 7 8 9 10 11 12 13 14 15 16 17 18 19 20 21 22 23 24 25 26 27 | | 28 29 30 31 |
| Due—February | 2 3 4 5 6 7 8 9 10 11 12 13 14 15 16 17 18 19 20 21 22 23 24 25 26 27 28 | March | 1 2 3 4 |

your object in breeding is merely to produce more dogs, you are strongly encouraged to reconsider your objective.

**WHEN TO BREED**

It is usually best to breed a bitch when she comes into her second or third season. Plan in advance the time of year which is best for you, taking into account your own schedule of activities (vacations, business trips, social engagements, and so on). Make sure you will be able to set aside plenty of time to assist with whelping of the newborn pups and caring for the dam and her litter for the next few weeks. At the very least, it probably will take an hour or so each day just to feed and clean up after the brood—but undoubtedly you will find it takes much longer if you stop to admire and play with the youngsters periodically! Refrain from selling the litter until it is at least six weeks old, keeping in mind that a litter of pups takes up a fair amount of space by then. It will be your responsibility to provide for them until they have been weaned from their mother, properly socialized, housebroken, and ready to go to new homes (unless you plan to keep them all). Hopefully, as strongly recommended, you will have already lined up buyers for the pups in advance of their arrival into this world.

**CHOOSING THE STUD**

You can plan to breed your female about six-and-one-half months after the start of her last season, although a variation of a

*Whelping box prepared with "pig rails," bars on either side of the box to prevent the bitch from rolling on the puppies.*

month or two either way is not unusual. Do some research into the various bloodlines within your breed and then choose a stud dog and make arrangements well in advance. If you are breeding for show stock, which will command higher prices than pet-quality animals, a mate should be chosen very carefully. He should complement any deficiencies (bad traits) that your female may have, and he should have a good show record or be the sire of show winners, if he is old enough to have proven himself. If possible, the bitch and stud should have several ancestors in common within the last two or three generations, as such combinations have been known, generally, to "click" best.

The owner of a stud dog usually charges a stud fee for use of the animal's services. This does not always guarantee a litter, but if she fails to conceive, chances are you may be able to breed your female to that stud again. In some instances the owner of the stud will agree to take a "first pick of the litter" in place of a fee. You should, of course, settle all details beforehand, including the possibility of a single puppy surviving, deciding the age at which the pup is to be taken, and so forth.

*Each puppy is delivered in a separate membranous sac. This sac must be removed by the bitch without delay—if not, the breeder must come immediately to the assistance of the pup.*

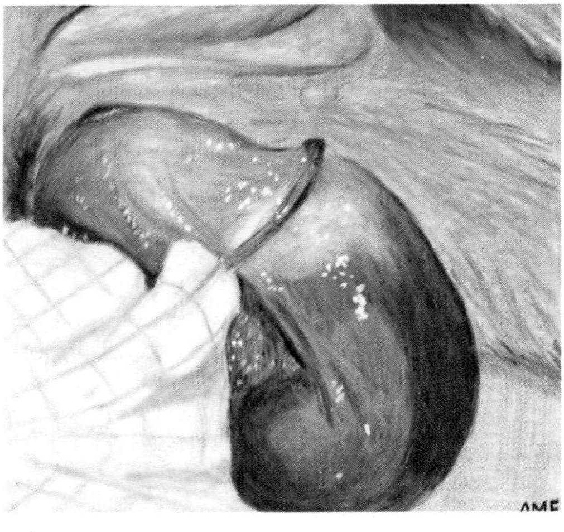

If you plan to raise a litter that will be sold exclusively as pets, and if you merely plan to make use of an available male (not a top stud dog), the most important selection point involves temperament. Make sure the dog is friendly, as well as healthy, because a bad disposition can be passed on to his puppies—and this is the worst of all traits in a dog destined to be a pet. If you are breeding pet-quality dogs, a "stud fee puppy," not necessarily the choice of the litter, is the usual payment. Don't breed indiscriminately; be sure you will be able to find good homes for each of the pups, or be sure you have the facilities to keep them yourself, *before* you plan to mate your dog.

### PREPARATION FOR BREEDING

Before you breed your female, make sure she is in good health. She should be neither too thin nor too fat. Any skin disease *must* be cured first so that it is not passed on to the puppies. If she has worms, she should be wormed before being bred or within three weeks after the mating. It is generally considered a good idea to revaccinate her against distemper and hepatitis before the puppies are born.

The female will probably be ready to breed twelve days after the first colored discharge appears. You can usually make arrangements to board her with the owner of the stud for a few days, to insure her being there at the proper time; or you can take her to be mated and bring her home the same day if you live near enough to the stud's owner. If the bitch still appears receptive she may be bred again two days later, just to make certain the mating was successful. However, some females never

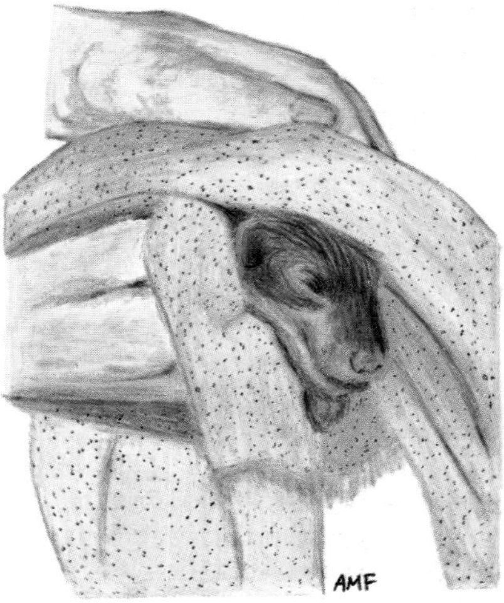


*Newborn pups are very susceptible to chills, so the breeder must dry the puppy off thoroughly and place it in a temperature-controlled puppy box.*

show signs of willingness, so it helps to have an experienced breeder on hand. In fact, you both may have to assist with the mating by holding the animals against each other to ensure the "tie" is not broken, that is, to make certain copulation takes place.

Usually the second day after the discharge changes color is the proper time to mate the bitch, and she may be bred for about three days following this time. For an additional week or so, she may have some discharge and attract other dogs by her odor; but she should not be bred.

Once she has been bred, keep her far from all other male dogs, as they have the capacity to impregnate her again and sire some of her puppies. This could prove disastrous where purebred puppies.

## THE FEMALE IN WHELP

You can expect the puppies nine weeks from the day of the mating, although 61 days is as common as 63. Gestation, that period when the pups are developing inside their mother, varies among individual bitches. During this time the female should receive normal care and exercise. If she was overweight at the start, don't increase her food right away; excess weight at whelping time can be a problem with some dogs. If she is on the thin side, however, supplement her meal or meals with a portion of milk and biscuit at noontime. This will help build her up and put weight on her.

You may want to add a mineral and vitamin supplement to her diet, on the advice of your veterinarian, since she will need an extra supply not only for herself but for the puppies growing inside her. As the mother's appetite increases, feed her more. During the last two weeks of pregnancy, the pups grow enormously and the mother will have little room for food and less of an appetite. She should be tempted with meat, liver, and milk, however.

As the female in whelp grows heavier, cut out violent exercise and jumping from her usual routine. Although a dog used to such activities will often play with the children or run around voluntarily,

*"Pooping" the puppies, or rubbing the bowels and genitals to stimulate elimination, may be necessary if the bitch doesn't tend to this herself.*

restrain her for her own sake.

A sign that whelping is imminent is the loss of hair around her breasts. This is nature's way of "clearing a path" so that the puppies will be able to find their source of nourishment. As parturition draws near, the breasts will have swelled with milk and the nipples will have enlarged and darkened to a rosy pink. If the hair in the breast region does not shed for some reason, you can easily cut it short with a pair of scissors or comb it out so that it does not mat and become a hindrance to the suckling pups later on.

*The breeder must actively partake in cleaning the pup after feedings. Hands-on contact serves as the initial step in socialization—accustoming the pup to his human family.*

## PREPARING FOR THE PUPPIES

Prepare a whelping box a few days before the puppies are due, and allow the mother to sleep there overnight or to spend some time in it during the day to become accustomed to it. This way she is less likely to try to have her pups under the front porch or in the middle of your bed. A variety of places will serve, such as the corner of your cellar or garage (provided these places are warm and dry). An unused room, such as a dimly lit spare bedroom, can also serve as the place for delivery. If the weather is warm, a large outdoor dog house will do, as long as it is well protected from rain, drafts, and the cold—and enclosed by fencing or a run. A whelping box serves to separate mother and puppies from visitors and other distractions. The walls should be high enough to restrain the puppies yet low enough to allow the mother to take a short respite from her brood after she has fed them. Four feet square is minimum size (for most dogs) and six-to-eight-inch high walls will keep the pups in until they begin to climb; then side walls should be built up so that the young ones cannot wander away from their nest. As the puppies grow, they really need more room anyway, so double the space with a very low partition down the middle of the box, and soon you will find them naturally housebreaking themselves. Puppies rarely relieve themselves where they sleep. Layers of newspapers spread over the whole area will make excellent bedding and be absorbent enough to keep the surface warm and dry. These should be removed daily and replaced with another thick layer. An old quilt or washable blanket makes better footing for the nursing puppies than slippery newspaper during the first week; this is also softer for the mother to lie on.

Be prepared for the actual whelping several days in advance. Usually the mother will tear up papers, refuse food, and become restless. These may be false alarms; the real test is her temperature, which will drop to below 100°F (38°C) about twelve hours before whelping. Take her

*Bottle-feeding may be necessary with particularly large litters or with a bitch who has become overly stressed or neglectful or whose milk has gone bad.*

temperature with a rectal thermometer, morning and evening, and usher her to her whelping box when her temperature goes down. Keep a close watch on her and make sure she stays safely indoors (or outdoors in a safe enclosure); if she is let outside, unleashed, or allowed to roam freely, she could wander off and start to go into labor. It is possible that she could whelp anywhere, and this could be unfortunate if she needs your assistance.

**WHELPING**

Usually little help is needed from you, but it is wise to stay close to be sure that the mother's lack of experience (if this is her first time) does not cause an unnecessary complication. Be ready to help when the first puppy arrives, for it could smother if she does not break the amniotic membrane enclosing it. She should tear open the sac and start licking the puppy, drying and stimulating it. Check to see that all fluids have

*Using simple genetic rules, an owner can predict to some degree the traits that the offspring of a given mating can exhibit. The six possible ways in which a pair of determiners can unite are illustrated on this Mendelian expectation chart. Ratios apply to expectancy over large numbers, except in lines 1, 2, and 6 where exact expectancy is realized in every litter.*

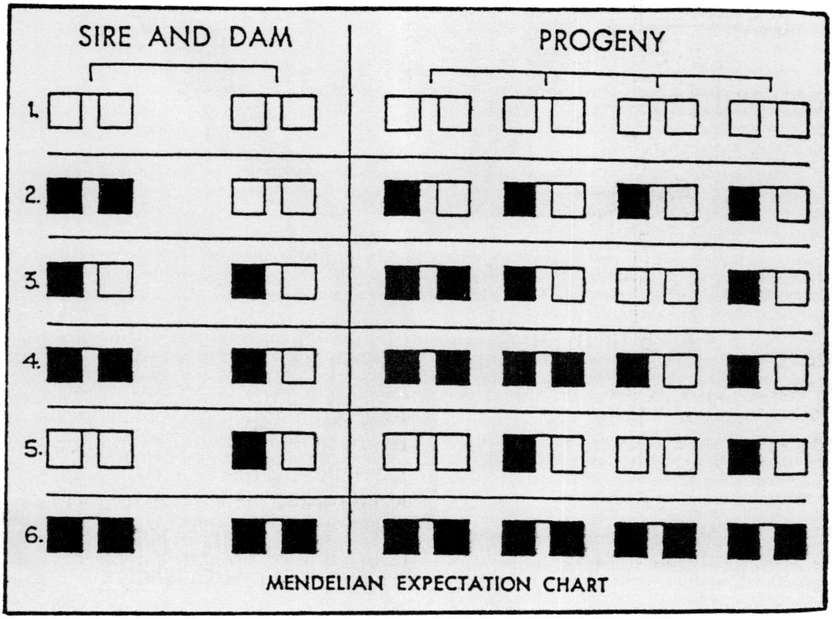

been cleared from the pup's nostrils and mouth after the mother has licked her youngster clean; otherwise the pup may have difficulty breathing. If the mother fails to tear open the sac and stimulate the newborn's breathing, you can do this yourself by tearing the sack with your hands and then gently rubbing the infant with a soft, rough towel. The afterbirth attached to the puppy by the long umbilical cord, should follow the birth of each puppy. Watch to be sure that each afterbirth is expelled, for the retention of this material can cause infection. In her instinct for cleanliness the mother will probably eat the afterbirth after severing the umbilical cord. One or two meals of this will not hurt her; they stimulate her milk supply, as well as labor, for remaining pups. However, eating too many afterbirths can make her lose appetite for the food she needs to feed her pups and regain her strength. So remove the rest of

*Prior to birth, the developing pups are housed in the horns of the uterus.*

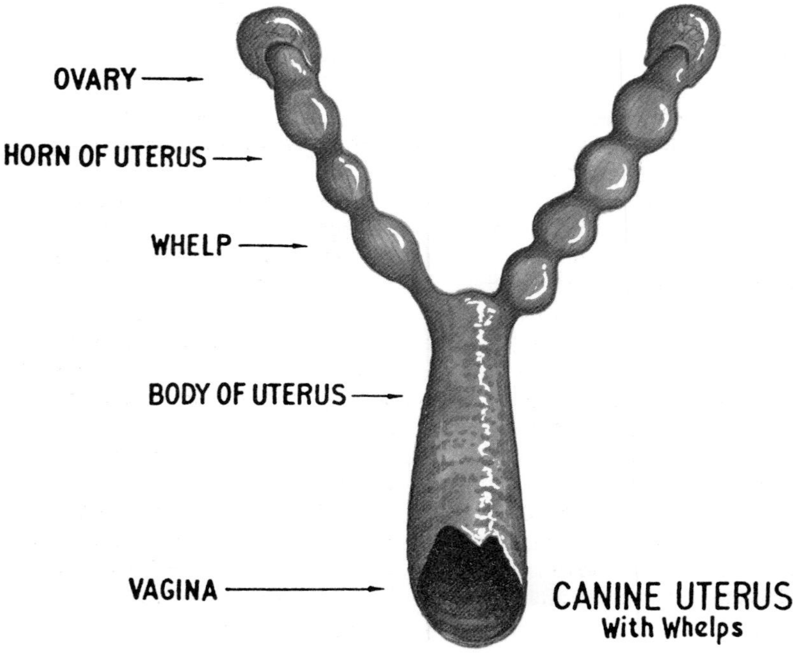

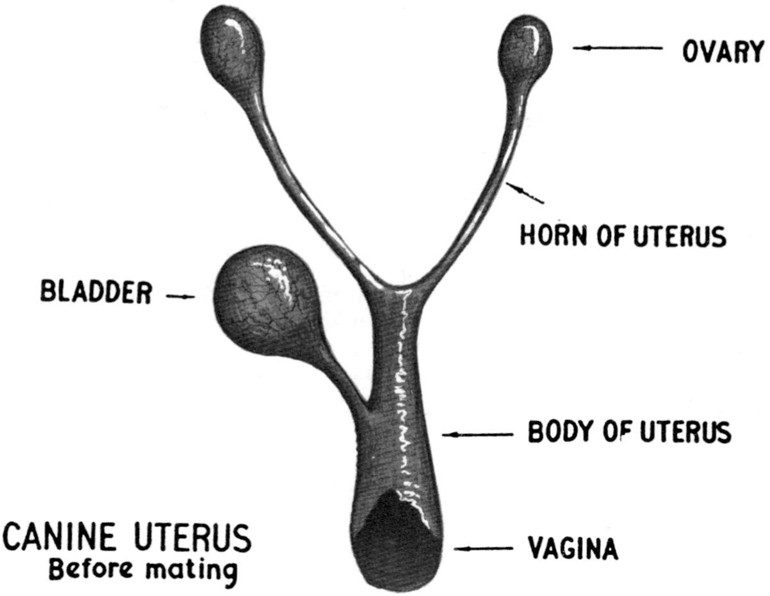


*The canine uterus is quite different from the human uterus. Besides the difference in shape, the canine uterus is designed to house an average of five to eight offspring.*

them, along with the wet newspapers, and keep the box dry and clean.

If the mother does not bite the cord or bites it too close to the puppy's body, take over the job to prevent an umbilical hernia. Tearing is recommended, but you can cut the cord, about two inches from the body, with a sawing motion with scissors that have been sterilized in alcohol. Then dip the end of the cut cord in a shallow dish of iodine; the cord will dry up and fall off in a few days.

The puppies should follow each other at intervals of not more than half an hour. If more time goes past and you are sure there are still pups to come, taking the mother for a brisk walk outside may start labor again. If she is actively straining without producing a puppy, the youngster may be presented backward, a so-called "breech" birth. Careful assistance with a well-lubricated finger to feel for the puppy or to ease it back may help, but never attempt to pull it out by force. This could cause serious damage, so seek the services of an expert—your veterinarian or an experienced breeder.

Even the best planned breeding can bear unexpected problems and complications. Therefore, do not rely solely on textbook knowledge of breeding and genetics. Experienced breeders and veterinarians will generally lend their words of wisdom—take full advantage of their generosity. Mere trial and error is no basis for any responsible breeding program.

If *anything* seems wrong during labor or parturition, waste no time in calling your veterinarian, who will examine the bitch and, if necessary, give her hormones to stimulate the birth of the remaining puppies. You may want his experience in whelping the litter even if all goes well. He will probably prefer to have the puppies born at his hospital rather than getting up in the middle of the night to come to your home. The mother would, no doubt, prefer to stay at home; but you can be sure she will get the best of care in a veterinary hospital. If the puppies are born at home, and all goes as it should, watch the mother carefully afterward. Within a day or two of the birth, it is wise to have the veterinarian check her and the pups to ensure that all is well.

Be sure each puppy finds a teat and starts nursing right away, as these first few meals supply colostral antibodies to help him fight disease. As soon

*Cells reproduce by a process called mitosis, in which the cells divide, forming two identical cells.*

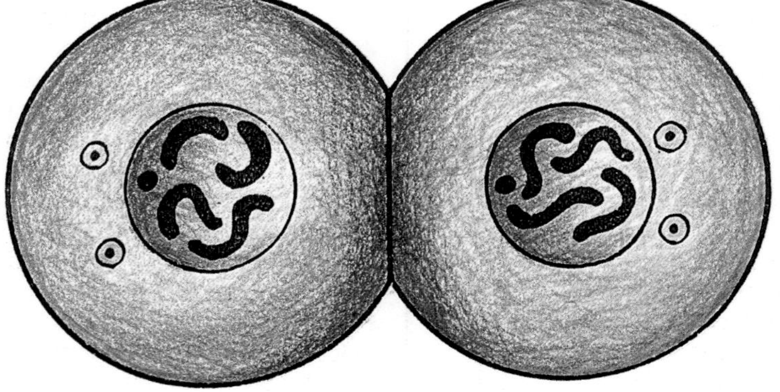

| PUPPY GROWTH AND BREEDER RESPONSIBILITY | |
|---|---|
| **AGE** | **REQUIRED CARE/EXPECTED DEVELOPMENT** |
| WEEKS 1–2 | Helpless; dam must provide constant care; owner must ensure warmth and cleanliness; puppy nurses, crawls, needs stimulation for elimination; sleeps 90% of time. |
| WEEKS 3–4 | Owner sustains optimum environment; puppy is alert, laps from bowl, takes first steps; defecates on its own; baby teeth emerge; barks, wags tail. |
| WEEKS 4–5 | Ambles, growls, and bites; play and interaction increase; human contact limited but essential; learning begins. |
| WEEKS 5–6 | Weaning; human socialization vital; pack order apparent; sex play; explores and sleeps less. |
| WEEKS 6–8 | Two to three daily meals; puppy accustomed to human family; breeder initiates housetraining; first veterinary visit; wary of the unknown. |

as he is dry, hold each puppy to a nipple for a good meal without competition. Then he may join his littermates in the whelping box, out of his mother's way while she continues giving birth. Keep a supply of puppy formula on hand for emergency feedings or later weaning. An alternative formula of evaporated milk, corn syrup, and a little water with egg yolk can be warmed and fed if necessary. A pet nurser kit is also a good thing to have on hand; these are available at local pet shops. A supplementary feeding often helps weak pups (those that may have difficulty nursing) over the hump. Keep track of birth weights and weekly readings thereafter; this will furnish an accurate record of the pups' growth and health, and the information will be valuable to your veterinarian.

### RAISING THE PUPPIES

After all the puppies have been born, take the mother outside for a walk and drink of water, and then return her to take care of her brood. She will probably not want to stay away for more than a minute or two for the first few weeks. Be sure to keep water available at all times and feed her milk or broth frequently, as she needs nourishment to produce milk. Encourage her to eat, with her favorite foods, until she seeks them of her own accord. She will soon develop a ravenous appetite and should have at least two large meals a day, with dry food available in addition. Your veterinarian can guide you on the finer points of nutrition as they apply to nursing dams.

Prepare a warm place to put the puppies after they are born to keep them dry and to help them to a good start in life. An electric heating pad, heat lamp or hot water bottle covered with flannel can be placed in the bottom of a cardboard box and near the mother so that she can see her puppies. She will usually allow you to help her care for the youngsters, but don't take them out of her sight. Let her handle things if your interference seems to make her nervous.

Be sure that all the puppies are getting enough to eat. If the mother sits or stands instead of lying still to nurse, the probable

*While in the womb, each pup is encased in an individual protective sac.*

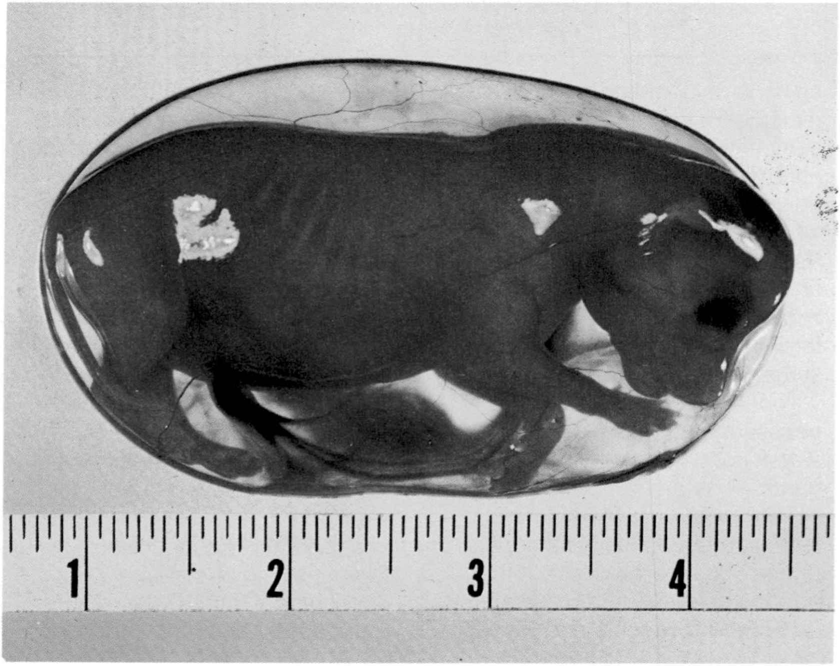

cause is scratching from the puppies' nails. You can remedy this by clipping them, as you would the bitch's, with a pet nail clipper. Manicure scissors also do for these tiny claws. Some breeders advise disposing of the smaller or weaker pups in a large litter, as the mother has trouble handling more than six or seven. You can help her out by preparing an extra puppy box or basket furnished with a heating pad and/or heating lamp and some bedding material. Leave half the litter with the mother and the other half in the extra box, changing off at two-hour intervals at first. Later you may exchange them less frequently, leaving them all together except during the day. Try supplementary feedings, too. As soon as their eyes open, at about two weeks, they will lap from a small dish.

*A puppy nurser kit is considered standard equipment by many breeders. These kits are available at your local pet shop.*

### WEANING THE PUPPIES

Normally the puppies should be completely weaned at five weeks, although you can start to feed them at three weeks. They will find it easier to lap semi-solid food than to drink milk at first, so mix baby cereal with whole or evaporated milk, warmed to body temperature, and offer it to the puppies in a saucer. Until they learn to lap it, it is best to feed one or two at a time because they are more likely to walk into it than to eat it. Hold the saucer at their chin level, and let them gather around, keeping paws off the dish. Cleaning with a damp sponge afterward prevents most of the cereal from sticking to the pups if the mother doesn't clean them up. Once they have gotten the idea, broth or babies' meat soup may be alternated with milk, and you can start them on finely chopped meat. At about four weeks, they will eat four meals a day and soon do without their mother entirely. Start them on canned dog food, or leave dry puppy food with them in a dish for self-feeding. Don't leave the water dish with them all the time; at this age everything is a play toy and they will use it as a wading pool. They can drink all they need if it is offered several times a day, after meals. As the puppies grow up, the mother will go into their "pen" only to nurse them, first sitting up and then standing. To dry up her milk supply completely, keep the mother away for longer periods; after a few days of part-time nursing she can stay away for even longer periods, and then permanently. The little milk left will be resorbed by her body.

The puppies may be put outside during the day, unless it is too cold or rainy, as soon as their eyes are open. They will benefit from the sunlight. A rubber mat or newspapers underneath will protect them from cold or dampness. As they mature, the pups can be let out for longer intervals, although you must provide them with a shelter at night or in bad weather. By now, cleaning up after the matured youngsters is a man-sized job, so put them out at least during the day and make your task easier. If you enclose them in a run or kennel, remember to clean it *daily*, as various parasites and other infectious organisms may be lurking if the quarters are kept dirty.

You can expect the pups to need at least one worming before they are ready to go to new homes. Before the pups are three weeks old, take a stool sample from each to your veterinarian. The vet can determine, by analyzing the stool, if any of the pups have worms—and if so, what kind of worms are present. If one puppy is infected, then all should be wormed as a preventive measure. Follow the veterinarian's advice; this also applies to vaccinations. You will want to vaccinate the pups at the earliest possible age. This way, the pups destined for new homes will be protected against some of the more debilitating canine diseases.

## THE DECISION TO SPAY OR NEUTER

If you decide not to use your male or female for breeding, or if you are obligated to have the animal altered based on an agreement made between you and the seller, make the necessary arrangements with your veterinarian as soon as possible. The surgery involved for both males and females is relatively simple and painless: males will be castrated and females will have their ovaries and uterus removed. In both

## REASONS TO SPAY/NEUTER DOGS

- **Reduces dog's need to roam.**
- **Reduces and/or eliminates certain reproductive cancers.**
- **Disburdens female dog of heat cycle and discomforts which accompany.**
- **Lessens dominance and mounting activity.**
- **Increases general lifespan of dog.**
- **Eliminates owner's concern of unwanted puppies, runaway stud dogs, stained furniture, nervous, and aggressive mood swings in pets.**
- **Relieves community of homeless dogs and property damage.**

cases, the operation does not alter their personalities; you will, however, notice that males will be less likely to roam, to get into fights with other male dogs, and to mount objects and people.

Your veterinarian can best determine at what age neutering or spaying should be done. With a young female dog, the operation may be somewhat more involved, and as a result be more costly; however, in the long run you will be glad you made the decision to have this done for your pet. After a night or two at the veterinarian's or an animal hospital, your bitch can be safely returned to your home. Her stitches will heal in a short time, and when they are removed, you will hardly notice her souvenir scar of the routine operation. Once she has been spayed, she no longer will be capable of having a litter of puppies.

Check with your city or town or with the local humane society for special programs that are available for pet owners. In many municipalities you can have your pet altered for just a small fee; the low price is meant to encourage pet owners to take advantage of this important means of birth control for their dogs. Pet adoption agencies and other animal welfare organizations can house only so many animals at one time, given the money, space, and other resources they have available. This is why pet owners are urged to have their pets altered, so that puppies resulting from accidental breedings won't end up being put to sleep as so many others have that are lost, stray, unwanted, or abandoned.

## Traveling With Your Pet

Most pets can be trained to become very good travellers provided you begin that training when your pet is still very young. Unfortunately, your puppy's first ride in the car is likely to be to the veterinarian's where, after a frightening, abrupt introduction to the noisy, jolting automobile, he is stabbed by horrible long needles. Is there any wonder that, in the future, he will run for cover whenever he hears you jingling your car keys?

**TRIPS BY CAR**

Familiarize your pet with your car by taking him to a nearby park or an open area where he can run about and enjoy himself. Thus, you will have associated the car with something pleasant. Throw a dog biscuit or favorite toy into his crate, which you have placed on the back seat of the car, in an effort to preoccupy him. Never allow your dog to ride uncrated, as there is nothing more dangerous than a playful pup jumping on his owner as he is driving. Your puppy should also keep his head inside a moving car as dust and debris could irritate his eyes and nostrils.

When you park your car and leave your pet inside, make certain that the windows are open at least two inches; dogs are particularly susceptible to heat exhaustion and the temperature in a parked car in the height of summer can reach over 120°F. Try to find a shady spot to park your car and return as soon as possible, as unscrupulous dognappers do exist who might pounce on your unsupervised pet. Of course, you must NEVER put your pet in the trunk of your car.

**LONG TRIPS**

When you prepare for a lengthy trip, make certain that you pack a few essential items for your canine companion: a blanket, a thermos of water, pet food, his food and water dishes, favorite toys, and any necessary medicine.

Do not give your pet a heavy meal before the trip but do ensure that he has a plentiful water supply. This will mean that you will have to break your journey several times so that he can relieve himself, but the rests and exercise will probably do you both good.

Most hotel chains in the United States welcome well-behaved pets but it is always wise to ask about their policy ahead of time when you make your reservation.

With early training and a little common sense, you and your pet will make excellent travelling companions *and* benefit from each other's company along the way.

**BOARDING YOUR DOG**

It may be necessary one day, however, to board your dog while you are on an extended vacation or business trip. In the United States, kennels which are members of the American Boarding Kennels Association should provide very good care for your pet. The A.B.K.A. is a nationwide non-profit organization established to promote high standards and professionalism in the pet-boarding industry.

Make certain to visit the kennels for an inspection before you board your dog. Examine the facilities, check the cleanliness of the stalls and exercise runs, talk to the owners about any special dietary or medical requirements your dog may have, look at the dogs staying there, and find out if there is a veterinarian on call. Also make your reservation well in advance, particularly if you plan to be away in the busy summer months or during the sometimes hectic holidays.

You can help your pet feel less homesick by taking his bed or favorite toy along. Finally, remember to leave an address or telephone number where you can be reached in case of an emergency.

*Always include the dog's favorite toys in his crate whenever you travel by car.*

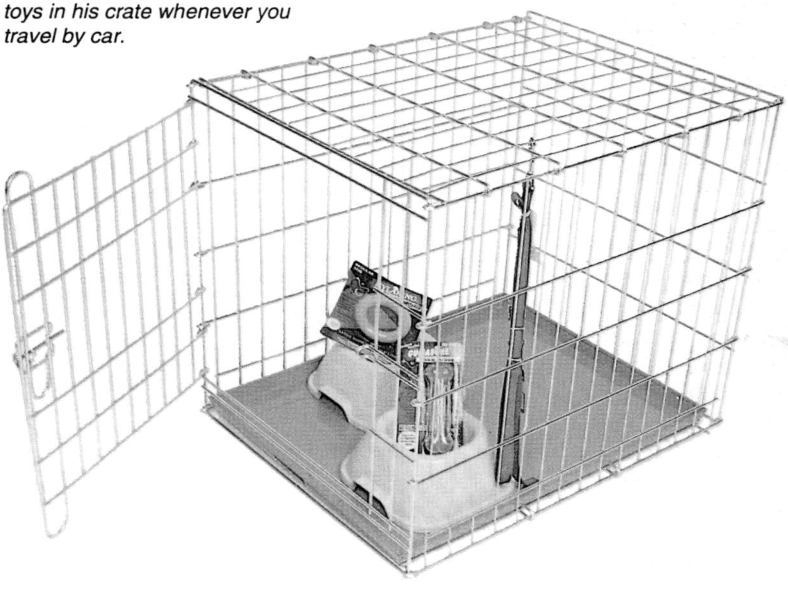

# Dog Books from t.f.h.

H-1016, 224 pp
135 photos

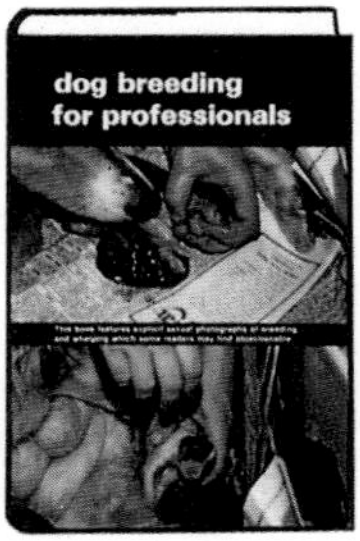


H-969, 224 pp
62 color photos

H-1061, 608 pp
Black/white photos

TS-101, 192 p
Over 100 pho

TW-102, 256 pp
Over 200 color

TW-113, 256 pp
200 color photos

H-962, 255 pp
Nearly 100 photos

SK-044, 64 pp
Over 50 color
photos

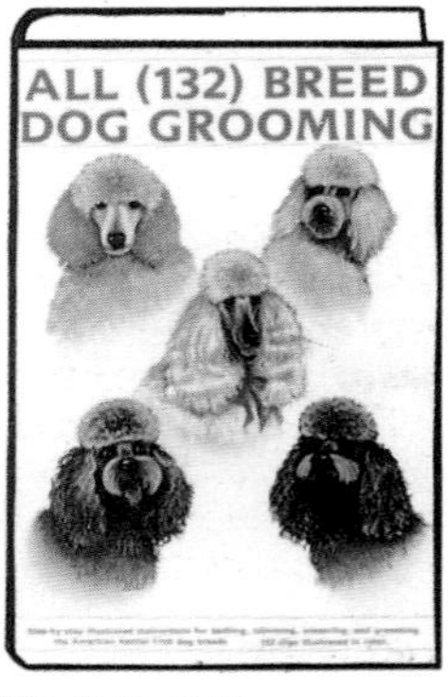


PS-872, 240 pp
178 color illustrations

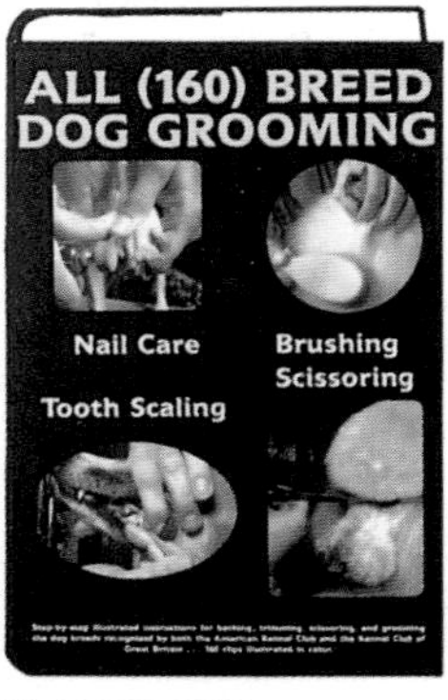


H-1095, 272 pp
Over 160 color illustrations

# All-Breed Dog Books From T.F.H.

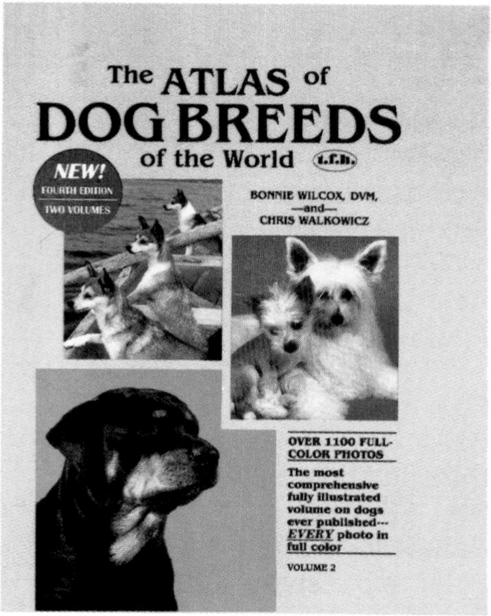


H-1091, 2 Vols., 912 pp
Over 1100 color photos

H-1106, 544 pp
Over 400 color photos

TS-175, 896 pp
Over 1300 color photos

The T.F.H. all-breed dog books are the most comprehensive and colorful of all dogs books available. The most famous of these recent publications, *The Atlas of Dog Breeds of the World,* written by Dr. Bonnie Wilcox and Chris Walkowicz, is now available as a two-volume set. Now in its fourth edition, the *Atlas* remains one of the most sought-after gift books and reference works in the dog world.

A very successful spinoff of the *Atlas* is *The Mini-Atlas of Dog Breeds,* written by Andrew De Prisco and James B. Johnson. This compact but comprehensive book has been praised and recommended by most national dog publications for its utility and reader-friendliness. The true field guide for dog lovers.

*Canine Lexicon* by the authors of the *Mini-Atlas* is an up-to-date encyclopedic dictionary for the dog person. It is the most complete single volume on the dog ever published covering more breeds than any other book as well as other relevant topics, including health, showing, training, breeding, anatomy, veterinary terms, and much more. No dog book before has ever offered this many stunning color photographs of all breeds, dog sports, and topics (over 1300 in full color).

# Index

076480

[redacted]

$2 Fine For Removing
the Bar Code Label!

WITHDRAWN